ISBN 978-1-333-65624-9
PIBN 10531885

# 1 MONTH OF
# FREE
# READING

## at

## www.ForgottenBooks.com

By purchasing this book you are eligible for one month membership to ForgottenBooks.com, giving you unlimited access to our entire collection of over 700,000 titles via our web site and mobile apps.

To claim your free month visit:

www.forgottenbooks.com/free531885

# THE

# MAGAZINE OF HISTORY

### WITH

## NOTES AND QUERIES

## 𝕰𝔵𝔱𝔯𝔞 𝔑𝔲𝔪𝔟𝔢𝔯—𝔑𝔬. 47

THE FEMALE REVIEW (LIFE OF DEBORAH SAMPSON, THE
FEMALE SOLDIER)  -   -   -   -   -   *H. Mann* (1797)
Revised by Rɴv. J. A. Vɪɴᴛᴏɴ, 1866

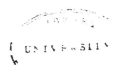

## WILLIAM ABBATT

TARRYTOWN                                           NEW YORK
1916

DEBORAH SAMPSON.

Published by H. Mann. 1797.

# The Female Review;

OR,

## LIFE OF DEBORAH SAMPSON.

# THE FEMALE SOLDIER

IN THE

WITH

## AN INTRODUCTION AND NOTES

BY

*JOHN ADAMS VINTON*

## J. K. WIGGIN & WM. PARSONS LUNT
M DCC LXVI

TARRYTOWN, NEW YORK
REPRINTED
WILLIAM ABBATT
1916
a Number 47 of THE MAGAZINE OF HISTORY WITH NOTES AND QUERIES.

## EDITOR'S PREFACE

THERE are a few cases known to history, of women serving as soldiers, without discovery of their sex, but all, save our heroine, were in foreign armies: she remains the only one known to our own army, until 1861-65, when according to Mrs. Livermore's "My Story of the War," there were many in the Union Army, by one unnamed authority almost four hundred—though of course none were enlisted if their sex was known.

It is admitted that there were two women in Washington's army who did soldier's work—Molly Pitcher of Monmouth, and Margaret Corbin of Fort Washington—But theirs was but a "service of occasion," and they were not regularly enlisted, as was Deborah Sampson.

Our readers will agree that it is most unfortunate that her own manuscript journal of her experiences was lost, and that Mr. Mann's verbose, grandiloquent and prosy production has to do duty in its place. We have felt obliged to reprint it in full—but it suffers greatly by comparison with almost any one of our other "EXTRAS"—particularly such a plain, straightforward, manly story as is Thomas Brown's "Plain Narrative"—(No. 4).

The original of 1797 is almost unprocurable and even the reprint of 1866, which we have followed, is very scarce.

We have been fortunate in discovering among the members of the D. A. R. one who is a direct descendant of Deborah Sampson, and from whom we have received the "family tree" which appears in the Appendix. This lady is Miss Amy Greer Thompson of New York, a great-great-granddaughter of our heroine, and the only member of the D. A. R. who belongs to the Society as representing a FEMALE SOLDIER. Others have been admitted as descendants of patriotic women, who rendered substantial services to the cause of Independence, but no one of them can point to a regularly-enlisted woman soldier as her ancestor.

We regret that the steel plate of Deborah Sampson's portrait cannot now be found, though known to be in Dedham a few years ago; and we are therefore obliged to be content with a half-tone reproduction from the original print.

# INTRODUCTION

(Sampson, Deborah.)   The Female Review: or, memoirs of an American young lady whose life and character are peculiarly distinguished—being a Continental soldier (for nearly three years) in the late American War, during which she performed the duties of every department into which she was called with punctual exactness, fidelity and honor. By a citizen of Massachusetts.   Portrait engraved by Graham, 4x6⅞.   Dedham: Printed by Nathaniel and Benjamin Heaton, for the author, 1797.                    $22.50

⁂The subject of this memoir was born at Plympton, Mass., in 1760.   Disguised as a man, she enlisted in the Revolutionary Army (Fourth Mass. Regiment), under the name of Robert Shurtleff, and was wounded in a skirmish at Tarrytown, N. Y.   She was also present at Yorktown.   After the war she married Benjamin Gannett of Sharon, Mass.

# INTRODUCTION

THE American Revolution was a great event. Thirteen feeble colonies, scattered along more than a thousand miles of sea-coast, and vulnerable at every point, dared to resist the colossal power of one of the oldest and strongest monarchies of the world. Without adequate preparation, without a general government, without a revenue, without a navy, and almost without an army, or the means of keeping an army together, they entered the fearful struggle, and, by the help of God, prevailed. All well-authenticated facts, even the most minute, connected with this great struggle, possess a deep and an enduring interest. Every individual history included in that great drama serves to help out and enlarge our idea of what was then transacted.

Viewed in this light, the story of Deborah Sampson will be found worthy of attentive consideration. It is sufficiently romantic in itself; but, considered as a tale of Revolutionary times, it is entitled to special regard. It affords, to some extend, a picture of those times, and opens before us scenes of trial and hardship, of patriotism and fortitude, that enable us better to conceive of that great conflict.

The general credit of the facts recorded in this volume cannot be shaken. It is sustained by tradition yet freshly existing in Middleborough and the vicinity; by the Records of the First Baptist Church in that town; by the Resolve of the Legislature of Massachusetts, in 1792; by the Records of the Pension Office of the United States; by the act of Congress, granting her pension to the heirs of Deborah Gannett; by the obituary notice published in the papers after her death; and, lastly, by the list of subscribers to "The Female Review." Many of these subscribers were highly respectable gentlemen, resident in Middleborough, Sharon, Stoughton, Dedham, Walpole, Wrentham, Providence, and other towns in the vicinity. Clergymen, physicians, lawyers, merchants, and other intelligent men, would not have subscribed for such a work, but for its substantial verity.

The story of our heroine has found a place, more or less enlarged, in "Allen's Biographical Dictionary," third edition; in Mrs. Sarah Josepha Hale's "Biography of Distinguished Women;" in Mrs. Elizabeth F. Ellet's "Women of the American Revolution;" and in some other publications.* In several of these volumes, minor inaccuracies may be found; but the main facts have never been called in question.

The editor remembers to have heard of this remarkable case full fifty years ago, in his childhood, when living in Braintree, midway between Boston and Middleborough. He has since made it a subject of careful and prolonged investigation.

The story, concisely told, is as follows: Deborah Sampson left her home in Middleborough, Mass., in May, 1782, being then in her twenty-second year. She assumed the masculine garb; enlisted as a Continental soldier; was mustered into the service at Worcester; joined the army at West Point; performed the duties of a soldier with more than ordinary alertness, gallantry, and fortitude; participated in several engagements, in one of which she was wounded; though mingling constantly with men, preserved her purity unsullied; suffered severe illness in a hospital in Philadelphia, where her sex was discovered; received an honorable discharge from the army at the close of the war, and returned to her relatives in Massachusetts.

These facts, and others connected with them, are set forth, with no inconsiderable amount of what was meant for embellishment, in "The Female Review," a small volume of 258 pages, 12mo., compiled by Herman Mann, and printed for him at Dedham, in

*Some years ago, as the editor has been informed, a volume made its appearance, professing to give memoirs of eminent colored women, and Deborah Sampson was claimed as one of the number!

1797. This book has long been out of print, and is now rarely to be met with. Considered merely as a composition, this volume does not rank high. The style is pompous and affected, the manner prolix and verbose. Throughout the volume, there is an evident straining after effect. Instead of presenting a simple narrative, "a round, unvarnished tale," the writer made a kind of novel, founded, indeed, on fact, but with additions of his own. He aimed at weaving a web of gaudy colors, which should strike strongly on the fancy of his readers. He introduces a great deal of extraneous matter, which serves only to fill out his pages, without at all helping forward the story. He proceeds with too little caution in his statements of fact, following, sometimes, the practice of Voltaire, who, when asked at the table of Frederick I., how he could allow himself in statements so variant from the truth, replied, "I write history to be read, not to be believed." This volume, however, has furnished, in great part, the material which has been used by most of the writers who have hitherto attempted to give an account of Deborah Sampson; and there can be no doubt that the well-authenticated facts of the case will repay a thoughtful considera tion.

To disengage what is true from what is of doubtful authority; to separate the real from the fictitious; to disentangle the facts from the fancies with which they have been mingled,—is the de sign of the present edition. But to draw the line accurately between the two has been found no easy matter.

It appears that the heroine, ten or twelve years after her return from the army, became acquainted with Mr. Mann, the original author; and some materials for the narrative were gathered, principally from her own lips, but in part also from some scattered memoranda of hers, from conversation with her relatives, from officers who knew her in the army, and from other sources. A journal, which she had constantly kept while in the service, was unfortunately lost with her trunk, in the passage by water, which

151

she attempted to make, from Elizabethtown, N. J., to New York, in a heavy gale, as she states, while on her return from a Western tour to the headquarters of the American army, in October, 1783. It was necessary, therefore, to rely chiefly on her memory; and, in regard to all important facts, this could hardly fail.

It seems, however, that both the writer and the heroine of "The Female Review," after the issue of that volume, became dissatisfied therewith: it seemed, even to them, a crude and imperfect sketch.   Many marks of carelessness, and of a want of due preparation, were too clearly seen; some things were untruly stated, and a general looseness of style and of sentiment was apparent. The resolution was formed, therefore, to prepare a worthier and more comely volume.   The writer had now become better acquainted with his subject, and possessed of an ampler stock of materials.   The book was therefore rewritten, with much enlargement in respect to facts, obtained from the heroine herself.   The memoir, thus revised, is said to have been carefully examined and fully approved by Mrs. Gannett, who exacted the promise, however, that it should not be printed till after her decease.   She died in 1827, and the author was thus relieved of the obligation.   But a severe and protracted illness, which resulted in the author's own death in 1833, prevented his fully completing the work.

The manuscript, after the author's death, fell into the hands of his son, to whom it appeared capable of still further improvement.   The younger Mann, therefore, took pains to remodel it thoroughly, omitting much of the extraneous matter, and making the heroine throughout to speak in the first person; thus giving more animation and directness to the narrative.   The dramatic style is employed wherever there is room for it.   We cannot avoid the impression that the MS. is dramatic throughout,—quite as much so as the historical plays of Shakespeare, while there can be no comparison in respect to artistic merit.   The manuscript memoir, or novel—whichever the reader pleases—was completed in

1850. It is a decided advance on "The Female Review" in style and manner, though still abounding in superfluous phrases, and containing much irrelevant matter. It exists only in a manuscript of 336 pages, and will probably never appear in print. All that is valuable in it has been incorporated in the present volume. The constant use of this document by the editor is an advantage which has not been enjoyed hitherto by any one who has given to the public an account of Deborah Sampson. He has thus been enabled to present a more full and, he trusts, a better history of this remarkable woman.

As the language of the manuscript memoir is susceptible of much improvement, I have not confined myself to the exact words. ThoughDeborah is ostensiblythe speaker, the words are Mr. Mann's. He speaks in her behalf, as her representative and interpreter. From the language employed by him, I have felt at liberty to de part whenever I thought the form of expression could be improved; dropping expletives, throwing off superfluous phrases, and changing one word for a better; new modelling whole sentences and para graphs for the sake of clearer and fuller expression; but never chang ing the idea. Even if I had Deborah's own words before me, the practice of good writers, in similar cases, would have warranted a careful and thorough revision.

The original work, however,—"The Female Review,"—is, in the following pages, literally and fully reprinted, that subscribers may possess the text as first printed in 1797. Copious notes are added wherever it seemed necessary, for the purpose of correcting erroneous statements, or presenting additional information.

From the nature of the case, there could be no other evidence in regard to most of the facts herein reported, but the statements of the heroine herself. Whether these statements can always be trusted, or whether, indeed, she ever made some of them, the reader must judge. The main thread of the story will undoubtedly hold

true, confirmed as it is by so many concurring testimonies. But
for some of the details of "The Female Review" and of the MS.
memoir, an easy faith is required.

Some years ago, my friend, Rev. Stillman Pratt of Middleborough, became interested in the story of Deborah Sampson, and
collected in that vicinity some facts not before published, which,
with other matter copied, without material alteration, from "The
Female Review," he gave to the world in his paper,"The Middleborough Gazette." The additional information thus obtained will
be found in the ensuing pages. In several instances, it is at vari-
ance with statements purporting to have been received from the
heroine.

The time when Deborah Sampson enlisted into the army has
been untruly stated. Mrs. Ellet, in her "Women of the Revolution," says she enlisted in October, 1778, when eighteen years of
age. This statement is copied by Dr. Allen, in his "Biographical
Dictionary," third edition. It is manifestly erroneous, for reasons
which will soon appear. "The Female Review," and Rev. Mr.
Pratt, who here copies from it, state that she enlisted in April,
1781. The MS. memoir, of which mention has already been made,
repeats the same statement. It is sustained by the following
document, which has just been obtained from the Pension Office
in Washington. It is a declaration made by Mrs. Gannett, under
oath, at the time when she relinquished her invalid pension and
received the benefit of the Act of Congress, passed March 18, 1818.

"United States:
    Massachusetts District.
    Deborah Gannett of Sharon, in the county of Norfolk, and district of Massachusetts,
a resident and native of the United States, and applicant for a pension from the United
States, under an act of Congress entitled, 'An Act to provide for certain persons engaged
in the land and naval service of the United States in the Revolutionary War,' maketh oath
that she served as a private soldier, under the name of Robert Shurtleff, in the war of the
Revolution, upwards of two years, in manner following, viz.: Enlisted in April, 1781, in
the company commanded by Captain George Webb, in the Massachusetts regiment commanded by Colonel Shepherd, and afterwards by Colonel Henry Jackson, and served in
said corps in Massachusetts and New York until November, 1783, when she was honorably

discharged in writing, which discharge is lost.  During the time of her service, she was at the capture of Lord Cornwallis, was wounded at Tarrytown, and now receives a pension from the United States, which pension she hereby relinquishes.  She is in such reduced circumstances as to require the aid of her country for her support.

DEBORAH GANNETT.

Massachusetts District, September 14, 1818."

The foregoing was copied, February 21, 1866, from the original, in the Pension Office in Washington.

At a later period, Mrs. Gannett applied to Congress for further aid, in a petition of which the following is a copy:—

"To the Hon. Senate and House of Representatives in Congress assembled.

The petition of Deborah Gannett of Sharon, in the county of Norfolk, and Commonwealth of Massachusetts, Humbly shews, That she served as a soldier in the Army of the United States, during the Revolutionary War; that she was wounded while in the service; and that while others were on the list of pensioners, and received their pensions soon after the termination of the war, she was not on the list of pensioners until the first of January, 1803, owing to the great disadvantage she was under to procure sufficient credentials which were necessary to lay before Congress.  She therefore prays that Congress would allow her at the rate of four dollars per month from the time that others in similar situations received their pensions, up to the first day of January, 1803.  And as in duty bound will ever pray.

Sharon, January 25, 1820."

DEBORAH GANNETT.

This petition was forwarded to Washington, to the care of Hon. Marcus Morton, then a representative in Congress from Massachusetts.  As appears by an indorsement thereon, it was referred, March 28, 1820, to the Committee on Pensions and Revolutionary Claims.  March 31, 1820, it was considered, but not allowed.  The original petition is now before me.

The following document was furnished on application from the editor:—

"DEPARTMENT OF THE INTERIOR,
Pension Office, February 13, 1866.

Sir,—In the matter of Deborah Gannett, about which you make certain inquiries, I have to state, that, on the 11th of March, 1805, she was allowed a pension of four dollars per month, as an invalid soldier of the war of the Revolution.  Her pension commenced January 1, 1803.  The name of the pensioner was inscribed upon the Massachusetts In-

◆

valid Pension Roll. In 1816, her pension was increased to six dollars and forty cents per month. On the 18th of March, 1818, Congress passed an Act, granting pensions of eight dollars per month to those soldiers who served, continuously, nine months and longer in the Continental line, and who were in need of the assistance of the country for support by reason of reduced circumstances. No person who was in the receipt of a pension could receive the benefit of this Act, unless he relinquished the pension he was receiving under former acts. In 1819, Deborah Gannett relinquished her Invalid Pension, and was pensioner under said Act of the 18th of March, 1818, at the rate of eight dollars per month, and drew said pension of eight dollars per month until March 4, 1827. She died in 1827. The papers upon which she was allowed her Invalid Pension were burned in 1814, when the War Office was burned by the British troops. The nature of her disability is not known, further than that she was severely wounded at Tarrytown. The soldier enlisted under the name of Robert Shertliff, in April, 1781, under Captain George Webb, in a regiment of the Massachusetts Continental line, commanded by Colonel Shepherd, and afterwards by Colonel Henry Jackson, and served until November, 1783, when she was honorably discharged. She was at the capture of Cornwallis.

Benjamin Gannett, the husband of the soldier, survived her as a widower, until 1837, when he died. On the 7th of July, 1838, Congress passed an Act, a Special Act (see Statutes at Large, vol 6, page 735), directing the Secretary of the Treasury to pay to the heirs of the soldier the sum of four hundred and sixty-six dollars and sixty-six cents, being at the rate of a pension of eighty dollars per annum from the 4th of March, 1831, to the 4th of January, 1837.

As this amount of four hundred and sixty-six dollars and sixty-six cents was paid at the Treasury, I am unable to state to whom, or when, it was paid. The foregoing embraces the information afforded by the files of this office, and, it is believed, every allowance made by law to Deborah Gannett, or her heirs.

I am yours, very respectfully,

JOSEPH H. BARRETT, *Commissioner.*"

Subjoined is a letter from the Secretary of War, in 1805, at the time of placing her name on the Invalid Pension Roll. The original, and also the original of the document which will immediately follow, are now in the possession of Mr. Jeremiah Colburn, of this city, who has kindly permitted the use of them by the editor:—

"War Department, 11 March, 1805.

Sir,—You are hereby apprised that Deborah Gannett, who served as a soldier in the Army of the United States, during the late Revolutionary War, and who was severely wounded therein, has this day been placed on the Pension List of the United States, at the rate of four dollars per month, to commence on the first day of January, 1803. You will be pleased to enter her name on your books, and pay her, or her legally authorized attorney, on application, accordingly.

I am, sir, very respectfully,

Your ob't servant,

H. DEARBORN."

Benjamin Austin, Jun., Esq., Boston.

Here is the first receipt given by Mrs. Gannett for her pension:—

"Commissioner's Office, April 10, 1805.

No. 12.

"Received of Benjamin Austin, jun., Agent for paying Invalid Pensioners belonging to the State of Massachusetts, One hundred and four dollars, 53⅓ cents, being for 26 months' and 4 days' Pension due to Deborah Gannett, from the first day of January, 1803, to the fourth day of March, 1805; for which I have signed duplicate Receipts.

DEBORAH GANNETT."

Dollars 104.53⅓."

The following is the Special Act of Congress referred to in the foregoing communication from the Pension Office:—

"An Act for the relief of the heirs of Deborah Gannett, a soldier of the Revolution, deceased:

Be it enacted, &c., That the Secretary of the Treasury be, and he is hereby, directed to pay, out of any money not otherwise appropriated, to the heirs of Deborah Gannett, a revolutionary soldier, and late the wife of Benjamin Gannett of Sharon, in the State of Massachusetts, now deceased, the sum of four hundred and sixty-six dollars and sixty-six cents, being an equivalent for a full pension of eighty dollars per annum, from the fourth day of March, 1831, to the decease of Benjamin Gannett, in January, 1837, as granted in certain cases to the widows of revolutionary soldiers by the Act passed the fourth day of July, 1836, entitled an Act granting half pay to widows or orphans where their husbands or fathers have died of wounds received in the military service of the United States, and for other purposes.

Approved July 7, 1838."

The subjoined Report of the Committee on Revolutionary Pensions, taken from Reports of Committees, Twenty-fifth Congress, 2d Session, Vol. 1., No. 172, January 31, 1837, adds some facts not elsewhere stated.

Mr. Wardwell, from the Committee on Revolutionary Pensions, made the following Report·—

"The Committee on Revolutionary Pensions, to which was referred the petition of Benjamin Gannett of Sharon, State of Massachusetts, report.

That the petitioner represents that he is the surviving husband of Deborah Gannett, to whom he was lawfully married on the 7th day of April, 1784; that she died on the 29th of April, 1827. He also states, that, in the early part of her life, the said Deborah enlisted as a soldier in the army of the Revolution, under the assumed name of Robert Shurtleff, where she faithfully served her country three years, and was honorably discharged in November, 1783; that, on account of a wound received in the service, she received a pension as an invalid, until the passage of the Act of 18th March, 1818; and that she received a full pension under the Act until her decease.   The petitioner further states, that the effects of the wound which she received followed her through life, and probably hastened her death.   The petitioner represents himself to be eighty-three years of age, infirm in health, and in indigent circumstances.   He states also that he has two daughters dependent on charity for support.   The petitioner prays that he may receive the amount of the pension of his wife, from the time of her decease, and that it may be continued to him till his death.

It appears, from a letter received from the Commissioner of Pensions, that Deborah Gannett, deceased, was placed on the Massachusetts roll of invalid pensioners, at $48 per annum, which was afterwards increased to $76.80 per annum.   This she relinquished, in 1818, for the benefit of the Act of March 18, 1918.   She was placed, under that law, at the rate of eight dollars per month, from the 14th September, 1818, which she received up to the 4th March, 1827.   It further appears, from said letter, that the papers containing evidence upon which the original pension was granted were burned in 1814, when the British troops invaded Washington, and destroyed the War Office, with its contents.

On the 14th September, 1818, the said Deborah made her declaration, under oath, that she served as a private soldier, under the name of Robert Shurtleff, in the war of the Revolution, upwards of two years, in manner following: Enlisted, in April, 1781, in a company commanded by Captain George Webb, in the Massachusetts regiment commanded by Colonel Shepherd*, and afterwards by Colonel Henry Jackson; that she served in Massachusetts and New York until November, 1783, when she was honorably discharged in writing, which discharge she had lost.   She was at the capture of Cornwallis, was wounded at Tarrytown, and, up to the date of her declaration, she received a pension therefor.

P. Parsons testifies, under oath, that she lived in the family of Benjamin Gannett more than forty-six years after he married Deborah Sampson; that she well knew that said Deborah was unable to perform any labor a great part of the time, in consequence of a wound she received, while in the American army, from a musket-ball lodged in her body, which was never extracted.   She also states that she saw Benjamin Gannett married to Deborah Sampson at his father's house in Sharon.

Benjamin Rhoads and Jeremiah Gould, the selectmen of the town of Sharon, in the State of Massachusetts, certify that they are acquainted with Benjamin Gannett, now living in said Sharon; that he is a man of upwards of eighty years of age; that he is destitute of property; that he has been an industrious man; that he was the husband of the late Deborah Gannett, deceased, who for a time received a pension from the United States for her military services during the Revolutionary War.

William Ellis, formerly a Senator in Congress, in a letter to the Hon. William Jackson, now a Representative in Congress, states that said Gannett has been a very upright, hard-laboring man; has brought up a large family, and is a poor man.   He further states, that he has long since been credibly informed that said Gannett had been subjected to heavy expenses for medical aid for his wife, the said Deborah, for twenty years or more, and before she received a pension under the Act of 1818, on account of wounds she received  in the United States service.

*William Shepard.

There are other certificates among the papers in this case, showing the physician's bill alone, for attendance on the said Deborah, to be more than six hundred dollars.

The Committee are aware that there is no Act of Congress which provides for any case like the present. The said Gannett was married after the termination of the war of the Revolution, and therefore does not come within the spirit of the third section of the Act of 4th July, 1836, granting pensions to widows in certain cases; and, were there nothing peculiar in this application which distinguishes it from all other applications for pensions, the Committee would at once reject the claim. But they believe they are warranted in saying that the whole history of the American Revolution records no case like this, and 'furnishes no other similar example of female heroism, fidelity, and courage.' The petitioner does not allege that he served in the war of the Revolution, and it does not appear by any evidence in the case that such was the fact. It is not, however, to be presumed that a female who took up arms in defence of her country, who served as a common soldier for nearly three years, and fought and bled for human liberty, would, immediately after the termination of the war, connect herself for life with a Tory or a traitor. He, indeed, was honored much by being the husband of such a wife; and as he has proved himself worthy of her, as he has sustained her through a long life of sickness and suffering, and as that sickness and suffering were occasioned by the wounds she received, and the hardships she endured in defence of the country; and as there cannot be a parallel case in all time to come, the Committee do not hesitate to grant relief.

They report a bill granting to the petitioner a pension of $80 per year from the 4th day of March, 1831, for and during his natural life."

The foregoing documents seem to prove conclusively that Deborah Sampson enlisted in the army in the month of April, 1781. The following documents prove as conclusively that she did not enlist till May, 1782. The reader will take notice that the preceding papers are all of a much later date than those that follow; and he will naturally be induced to ask why the statement that the enlistment was in April, 1781, was not inserted in so important a document as that which we shall now copy, and which was made when the facts of the case were so recent.

In January, 1792, Deborah Gannett, formerly Deborah Sampson, signed a petition to the Legislature of Massachusetts, of which the following is an exact copy:—

"To His Excellency the Governor, the Honourable Senate, and the Honourable House of Representatives, in General Court assembled, this Eleventh day of January 1792.
    The Memorial of Deborah Gannet
Humbly Sheweth, that your Memorialist from Zeal for the good of her Country was induc'd, and by the name of Robert Shirtliff did, on May 20, 1782, Inlist as a Soldier in the

Continental Service, for Three Years, into the 4<sup>th</sup> Regiment, Col? Shepard's, (afterwards Col? Jackson's) in Cap.<sup>t</sup> George Webb's Compy. & was muster'd at Worcester, by Cap.<sup>t</sup> Eliphalet Thorp of Dedham, the 23<sup>d</sup> of the same Month, & went to the Camp, under the Command of Sergeant Gambel, & was constant & faithful in doing Duty, with other Soldiers, & was engag'd with the Enemy at Tarry Town New York, & was wounded there by the Enemy, & continued in Service untill discharg'd, by General Knox at West Point, October 25, 1783. - - - - - Your Memorialist has made some Application to receive pay for her services in the Army, but being a Female, & not knowing the proper steps to be taken to get pay for her services, has hitherto not receiv'd one farthing for her services: whether it has been occasion'd by the fault of Officers in making up the Rolls, or whether Effrican Hamlin paymaster to the 4<sup>th</sup> regiment, has carried off the papers, &c. your Memorialist cannot say: but your Memorialist prays this Honourable Court to consider the Justness of her Claim, & Grant her pay as a good soldier; and your Memorialist as in Duty bound shall ever pray."

*Deborah Gannett*

The foregoing petition was presented to the House of Representatives, and by them referred to a committee, consisting of Dr. William Eustis of Boston (afterwards Governor), Benjamin Hitchborn of Dorchester, and James Sproat of Middleborough. This Committee reported favorably on the petition, and consequently the following Resolve was passed:—

"Commonwealth of Massachusetts:

House of Representatives, January 19<sup>th</sup>, 1792.

On the petition of Deborah Gannet, praying compensation for services performed in the late Army of the United States.

Whereas it appears to this Court that the said Deborah Gannet inlisted, under the name of Robert Shirtliff, in Capt.<sup>t</sup> Webb's company, in the 4<sup>th</sup> Massachusetts Regiment on May 20, 1782, and did actually perform the duty of a soldier in the late Army of the United States to the 23<sup>d</sup> day of October 1783, for which she has received no compensation:

And whereas it further appears that the said Deborah exhibited an extraordinary instance of female heroism by discharging the duties of a faithful, gallant soldier, and at the same time preserving the virtue & chastity of her sex unsuspected and unblemished, & was discharged from the service with a fair & honorable character. Therefore—

Resolved, That the Treasurer of this Commonwealth be and he hereby is directed to issue his note to the said Deborah for the sum of thirty-four pounds, bearing interest from October 23, 1783.

Sent up for Concurrence.                                    D. COBB, *Speaker.*

In Senate, Jan<sup>y</sup> 20, 1792. Read and concurred.

SAM<sup>L.</sup> PHILLIPS, *President.*

Approved,

JOHN HANCOCK."

160

Connected with the foregoing papers is the following:—

Boston, Aug⁺ 1, 1786.

To whom it may concern.

These may certify that Robert Shurtliff was a soldier in my Regiment in the Continental army for the town of Uxbridge in the Commonwealth of Massachusetts & was inlisted for the term of three years:—that he had the confidence of his officers and did his duty as a faithful and good soldier, and was honorably discharged the army of the United States.

HENRY JACKSON,
*Late Col. in the American Army."*

A true copy of the original delivered said Shurtliff.

Attest.
JOHN AVERY JUN^R *Sec'y."*

The subjoined certificate accompanies the preceding papers:—

"Dedham, Decm⁺ 10, 1791.

This Certifies that Mrs. Deborah Gannet inlisted as a soldier on May y^e 20^th 1782 for three years and was Muster'd y^e 23^d of y^e Same Month at Worcester and sent on to Camp soon after and as I have been inform'd did the Duty of a Good Soldier.

"P⁺ ELIPH^T THORP, *Cap⁺ 7^th M. Reg⁺ M. Master*

N. B.   Robert Shirtleff was y^e Name by which M^rs Gannet inlisted and Muster^d"

The four documents immediately preceding are on file in the office of the Secretary of the Commonwealth of Massachusetts, and were copied exactly by the editor from the originals. They are all in one fold, and are endorsed—

"Resolve on the petition of Deborah Gannet, granting her £34 for services in the late Continental Army.   Jan^y 20, 1792."

The sum granted, £34, was equivalent to one hundred dollars, and a small fraction over.

In reference to these documents, a strict regard to truth compels us to offer the following observations:—

1.   Deborah Gannett, formerly Sampson, the heroine of our story, in presenting to the Legislature a petition for compensation as a soldier, must have made the utmost of her case.   If she had been a soldier in 1778, or in 1781, and especially if she had been a sharer in the glorious campaign which ended in the surrender of

Cornwallis, she would doubtless have said so; and, if such were the fact, she could easily have proved it. But the petition of 1792 says nothing of this sort.

2. As we know from her own statement in this petition that she enlisted in May, 1782, it is scarcely possible that she could have enlisted in 1781, because, in that case, she must have enlisted for one year only. But the practice of short enlistments, which had nearly proved fatal to the American cause in the autumn and winter of 1776, had, in 1781, long been abandoned. Moreover, it appears, from the "Continental Army Books,"* in the office of the Secretary of the Commonwealth, that all the men in Colonel Shepard's regiment, as well as in the other regiments of the Massachusetts line, were enlisted "for three years, or during the war."

3. She could not have enlisted in 1778, as Mrs. Ellet affirms, because, in that case, the "Continental Army Books," just mentioned, would contain the name of Robert Shirtliff. But they do not contain it. The name of Robert Shirtliff appears in the "List of Final Settlement," a volume in the office of the said Secretary, containing the names of the soldiers who were discharged in 1783. Opposite to his name is number 40066, referring to documents sent to the War Office at Washington, and destroyed when the War Office was burned in 1814.

4. Though the petition of Mrs. Gannett affirms that she enlisted for three years, and though the same statement is made in the certificates of Colonel Jackson and Captain Thorp, yet it does not follow that she served three years. She says that she was discharged in October, 1783. Her actual service, therefore, if we may believe her statement in the petition of 1792, was limited to one year and five months.

5. Some of the statements, both of "The Female Review"

*They contain the names of all who served in the Massachusetts regiments from 1777 to 1780, and the amounts due them respectively.

and of the MS. memoir, seem incredible. In both of these docu
ments, especially in the latter, we are conducted, with great full
ness of detail, through the campaign of 1781; the siege of Yorktown; the hard work in the trenches; the taking of two formidable
British redoubts by storming parties; and the final surrender of
the hostile forces: and Deborah Sampson, we are assured, was a
sharer in these stirring scenes. Had she forgotten her part in
those memorable transactions when she presented her petition to
the Legislature of Massachusetts, only ten years afterwards?

Further to confirm what we have now said, we offer an extract
from the Records of the First Baptist Church in Middleborough;
of which Church, as appears by those Records, Deborah was received a member in November, 1780:—

"September 3, 1782. The Church took action as follows:

The Church consider'd the case of Deborah Sampson, a member of this Church, who
last Spring was accused of dressing in men's clothes, and enlisting as a Soldier in the Army,
and altho she was not convicted, yet was strongly suspected of being guilty, and for some
time before behaved very loose and unchristian like, and at last left our parts in a suden
maner, and it is not known among us where she is gone, and after considerable discourse,
it appeard that as several bretheren had labour'd with her before she went away, without
obtaining satisfaction, concluded it is the Church's duty to withdraw fellowship until
she returns and makes Christian satisfaction."

A vote to "withdraw fellowship" is equivalent to a vote of
excommunication. It does not appear that Deborah was ever
restored to the communion of that church, or of any other.

From this extract it seems evident that she did not "dress in
men's clothes, and enlist as a soldier in the army," till the spring
of 1782. If so, she did not enlist till the war was substnatially
over. The surrender of Cornwallis, in October, 1781, virtually
closed the contest. No military operations, of any importance,
were, after that event, undertaken on either side.

It must be confessed, however, that the case is not wholly
free from difficulty. The heroine of the story, who best knew the
facts of the case, has given her testimony on both sides of the ques-

tion.  In January, 1792, she makes a positive statement that she
enlisted in May, 1782, and is altogether silent about her being
present at the siege of Yorktown.  In September, 1818, twenty-
six years later, she affirms, under oath, that she enlisted in April,
1781, and was at the capture of Cornwallis (see p. xvi.).  The statements subsequently made in the document obtained from the Pen
sion Office (p. xix.), and in the Report of the Committee on Revolutionary Pensions (p. xxi), that her enlistment was in April, 1781,
are evidently derived only from her declaration, in 1818, just mentioned, which was clearly an after-thought.  The reader is left
to judge as to the probabilities of the case.

After making all needful allowance for these conflicting statements, and for the exaggerations of the book before us, enough re
mains to invest the story of Deborah Sampson with a strange and a
peculiar interest.  She was certainly a woman of very marked and
decided character.  She is entitled, as no other female is, to be
denominated "the heroine of the American Revolution."  Other
women, during that eventful struggle, were patriotic, and brave,
and courageous.  Margaret Corbin, with manly fortitude, filled
the place of her husband, who was killed by her side while serving
a piece of artillery, at the attack on Fort Washington, and for this
act of female heroism received a pension from Congress.  The story
of the gunner's wife* is not forgotten, who took her husband's post
when he was killed at the battle of Monmouth, and did such execution, that, after the engagement, she was rewarded with a commission.  Mrs. Ellet has supplied a long list of other "women of
the Revolution," who rendered important services to their country's cause.  Deborah Sampson alone, so far as we know, entered
the ranks as a common soldier, and, during two entire campaigns,
performed the arduous duties of such a position.  The most remarkable feature of the case is, that during those entire campaigns, while mingling constantly with men, night and day, in all

*Molly Pitcher.

their exercises, through so many months, she maintained her virtue unsullied, so that her sex was not even suspected. That such was the fact, we are assured by the Resolve of the Legislature of Massachusetts, and by many other concurrent testimonies. Her example in enlisting as a soldier is certainly not to be commended to the imitation of our fair countrywomen; but her inflexible resolution and firm self-control, after she enlisted, are deserving of high praise. Indeed, we know not whether, in all respects, the world's history affords a parallel to the case. Women are always found in camps, sometimes in great numbers; not always, however, for worthy ends. Women in men's clothes were found dead at Waterloo, and on other battlefields in Europe. Many remarkable instances of female courage and heroism occurred in our late civil war. Several ladies of culture and refinement exposed themselves to far greater risks, in the "secret service," both of the Federal Government and of the rebel army, than were assumed by our heroine.* Woman, we well know, may have a manly heart. Many have excelled in manly qualities and in manly exercises, often bearing off the palm from the stronger sex.

*Mrs. Smith, wife of Captain Smith of the Army of the Cumberland, left a life of luxury for the utmost hardships of the camp and the field, to accompany her husband, and serve the cause of the Union. She distinguished herself as a scout, and performed several extremely bold exploits. She once captured, single-handed, three rebel soldiers, with their horses, which they were leading to water. At another time she defeated a plan of the rebels for the capture of her husband's company and the regiment, by a ride of more than thirty miles on a stormy night, encountering many dangers on the way. Pauline Cushman, an actress well known in the West, a woman of great energy and fine personal appearance, rendered very effective and valuable aid to the operations of the Western armies. Both as a scout and as a spy, she was engaged in many daring adventures in the cause of the Union, unravelling, by her uncommon talents, more than one deeply-laid plot of the rebels, and bringing to the leaders of our armies much useful information from the camps of the enemy. Mrs. Brownell,* wife of Orderly-sergeant R. S. Brownell, of the Fifth Rhode Island Regiment, accompanied her husband to the war. She was at the battles of Bull Run, of Roanoke Island, and of Newbern, exhibiting great presence of mind, attending to the wounded, and encouraging the soldiers by her fortitude. When a standard bearer fell she seized the banner, and, carrying it across the field, received a wound.—[ *U. S. Ser. Mag.*, September, 1865.]

*Died 1914, at New York.

Ducit Amazonidum lunatis agmina peltis
Penthesilea furens, mediisque in millibus ardet,
Aurea subnectens exsertæ cingula mammæ
Bellatrix, audetque viris concurrere virgo.

But Penthesilea and the Amazons never existed, save in epic poetry; and the story of Semiramis, long believed, is now fully exploded. Boadicea, the British warrior-queen, "rushed to battle, fought, and died." Jane of Montfort, clad in complete armor, performed prodigies of valor, and, in her little castle of Hennebon, successfully withstood the arms of France. Joan of Arc,

"The maid with helméd head,
Like a war-goddess, fair and terrible,"

retrieved the desperate affairs of the French realm.. Elizabeth of England, and Catharine of Russia, nearer our own times, extended their influence and their renown into distant regions.

The following extract of a letter from Hon. William Ellis, formerly a Senator in Congress, may form a fitting conclusion to these introductory remarks. It was furnished to the editor by Hon. Peter Force of Washington, D. C., and is dated Dedham, February 4, 1837:—

"From my own acquaintance with Deborah Gannett, I can truly say that she was a woman of uncommon native intellect and force of character. It happens that I have several connections who reside in the immediate neighborhood where Mrs. Gannett lived and died; and I have never heard from them, or any other source, any suggestions against the character of this heroine. Her stature was erect, and a little taller than the average height of females. Her countenance and voice were feminine; but she conversed with such ease on the subject of theology, on political subjects, and military tactics, that her manner would seem to be masculine. I recollect that it once occurred to my mind that her manner of conversation on any subject embraced that kind of demonstrative, illustrative style which we admire in the able diplomatist."

TO THE

*P A T R O N S* AND *F R I E N D S*

OF

C O L U M B I A's  C A U S E;

THE  F E M A L E   R E V I E W

*Is DEDICATED:*

THOUGH not with intentions to encourage the like paradigm of Female Enterprise—but because such a thing, in the course of nature, has occurred; and because every circumstance, whether natural, artificial, or accidental, that has been made conducive to the promotion of our Independence, Peace, and Prosperity—all through Divine Aid, must be sacredly remembered and extolled by every one, who solicits the Perpetuity of these invaluable Blessings.

THE AUTHOR.

# PREFACE.

THERE are but two degrees in the characters of mankind that seem to arrest the attention of the public. The first is that of him who is the most distinguished in laudable and virtuous achievements, or in the promotion of general good. The second, that of him who has arrived to the greatest pitch in vice and wickedness.

Notwithstanding these characters exhibit the greatest contrast among mankind, it is not doubted but each, judiciously and properly managed, may render essential service. Whilst the former ever demands our love and imitation, the other should serve to fortify our minds against its own attacks—exciting only our pity and detestation. This is the only method, perhaps, by which good may be said to come out of evil.

My first business, then, with the public, is to inform them, that the Female who is the subject of the following Memoirs, does not only exist in theory and imagination, but in reality. And were she not already known to the public, I might take pride in being the first to divulge—a distinguished Character. Columbia has given her birth; and I *estimate her natural source too highly to presume she is dishonoured in the acknowledgment of such an offspring.

However erroneous this idea may be deemed, I shall here state only two general traits in her life to corroborate its truth. The criterion will still remain to be formed by a candid and impartial public.

She was born and educated in humble obscurity—distinguished during her minority, only by unusual propensities for learning, and few opportunities to obtain the inestimable prize. At the age of eighteen she stepped forward upon a more exalted stage of action.†

*According to the *Errata* in the original, this should read "I should estimate her natural source too meanly, to presume," etc.—[ED.]

†The heroine was in her twenty-second year when "she stepped forward upon a more exalted stage of action."—EDITOR.

She found Columbia, her common parent, enveloped and distracted with confusion, anguish and war. She commiserated, as well as participated, her sufferings. And as a proof of her fidelity and filial attachment, she voluntarily offered her services in the character of a Continental Soldier in defence of her cause; by which she seemed resolved to rescue the rest of her brothers and sisters from that flagrant destruction, which, every instant, seemed ready to bury them in one general ruin; or to perish, a noble sacrifice, in the attempt.

Having noted the leading traits of this illustrious Fair, I hasten to give a concise account of the design and execution of the work.

Justice, in the first place, demands that I should mention the reluctance with which she has consented to the publication of this Review of her life. Though it has become more fashionable, in these days of liberty and liberality, to publish the lives of illustrious persons, yet she refused the solicitations of a number of literary characters to publish her own, till after her exit. She is not a stickler for tradition; yet this is against her.

About sixteen months ago, by desire of a friend, I made her a visit for this purpose. She did not positively discard my request. Being indisposed, she said, should she recover, if I would again be at the trouble to call on her, she would in the interim take advice, consult matters with herself and come to a final decision. This was the first of my acquaintance with her.

In a few weeks, I again waited on her. Having critically weighed her own feelings, and wishing to gratify the curiosity of many of whom she had taken advice—with extreme modesty and trembling dissidence, she consented to take a public Review of the most material circumstances and events of her life. She relies on that candor and impartiality from the public that now attend the detail of her Memoirs.

I intended to have executed this work at leisure; as indeed I have. I had no other way; as the materials were mostly to be collected. This, with other pressing avocations in life, brings me under the necessity to apologize to my worthy Patrons, for the delay of its publication a few weeks longer than the intended time.

Sensibly impressed with the idea that every subject intended for public contemplation should be managed with intentions to promote general good, I have, in every instance, in the *Female Review*, indefatigably labored for this important end. But perhaps I differ from most biographers in this respect. I have taken liberty to intersperse, through the whole, a series of moral reflections, and have attempted some literary and historical information. However singular this is, I have the vanity to think it will not be deemed useless.

As an impartial writer, I am bound to handle these Memoirs in a disinterested manner. But where a total sacrifice of truth does not forbid, I take pride in publicly avowing, in this place, my desire (as every one ought) to extol virtue, rather than give the least countenance to vice under any name, pretext or sanction. Both may be represented and discussed—Vice exposed—Virtue cherished, revered and extolled.

The authorities upon which I have ventured for the support of facts related in the following Memoirs, are not merely the words of the lady's own mouth. They have been detailed to me by persons of veracity and notoriety, who are personally, acquainted with the circumstances. But I particularly refer my readers to the documents accompanying the appendix.

It would be almost incredibly strange, should no idle, capricious and even calumnious tale take rise with respect to the reputation of the female, distinguished as she is, who is the subject of these sheets. Being aware of this, she has already anticipated, and perhaps, in some measure experienced it. Her precaution now is, to

prepare for the worst.  She dreads no censure—no lash of aspersion more than that of the judicious and virtuous.  My own wishes
are in this respect, as in all others, that truth, candor and charity
may be our ruling principles.  When we seriously consider the
horrors, dangers and general fare of war—that it is unavoidably
attended with many irregularities, to which she was exposed in
common with the rest; and yet, if it be found that decorum and
propriety of conduct predominated in her general pursuits, we
may bear to palliate a few foibles, from which we, even in our most
sequestered, happy and serene retirements, are not, always, exempt.

There are but two sides to a person's character any more than
there are to his garments—the dark and bright.  In many researches in the *Female Review*, though I have decidedly declared
my choice for virtuous and laudable actions, yet, I have endeavoured to pay proper attention to their opponents, when they happened
to make me visits.  But if I must hereafter suffer the lash of aspersion from either sex for having shown partiality, I shall rejoice
in the conscientious satisfaction of having given the preference to
the bright side.

Perhaps there is not one new idea, in the course of these Memoirs, advanced or hinted on the important business of education.
But should I be so successful, as to rouse the minds and excite the
attention of the inattentive to those principles which have before
been deemed useful  I shall esteem it the most agreeable and ample
compensation for my endeavours.

Suspicious, from my first engagement, that the *Female Review* would be a subject as delicate, especially for the Ladies, as
it is different from their pursuits, I have studiously endeavored
to meliorate every circumstance that might seem too much tinctured with the rougher, masculine virtues.  This, however, has
not been attempted with the duplicity of a facetious courtier; but
with a diction softened and comported to the taste of the vir-

tuous female. And although I am a well-wisher to their whole circle, it is the case of this class, only, I wish to promote.

I cannot disapprove their vehement attachment to many novels—even to the productions of our own soil. Whilst they touch the passions with all that is captivating and agreeable, they inspire manly thoughts and irresistibly gain our assent to virtue. As the peculiar events that have given rise to the *Female Review* stand without a rival in American annals, I also hope my endeavours to render it agreeably entertaining and useful to them may not prove fallacious nor in vain. I readily yield the palm of style to the rapturous and melting expressions of the novelist: But I must vie with him in one respect:—What he has painted in embryo, I have represented in expansion.

This gallant Heroine has been reared under our own foster-age: and to reject her now would be disowning a providential circumstance in our revolutionary epoch, which the annals of time must perpetuate.

Europe has exhibited its chivalry and wonders. It now remains for America to do the same: And perhaps the most singular is already past—her beginning in infancy! It is a wonder, but a truth full of satisfaction, that North America has become free and independent. But a few years have elapsed since this memorable era; yet even the face of nature has assumed a new and beautiful aspect. Under the fostering powerful hands of industry and economy, art and science have taken a rapid growth. The wreath of Virtue has sprung up; and Liberty delights in twining it round her votary's brow.

Happy in the possession of such a Source for improvement, we should be barbarians to ourselves to be inattentive to its promotion. Whilst other nations may envy us the enjoyment of such distinguished rights and felicity Heaven grant we may vie with them only for that, which dignifies and promotes the character of Man.

MASSACHUSETTS, July, 1797.

# THE

# FEMALE REVIEW:

OR,

## MEMOIRS

OF AN

# AMERICAN YOUNG LADY;

WHOSE LIFE AND CHARACTER ARE PECULIARLY DISTIN-
GUISHED — BEING A CONTINENTAL SOLDIER, FOR NEARLY
THREE YEARS, IN THE LATE AMERICAN WAR.

DURING WHICH TIME,
SHE PERFORMED THE DUTIES OF EVERY DEPARTMENT,
INTO WHICH SHE WAS CALLED, WITH PUNCTUAL EXACTNESS,
FIDELITY AND HONOR, AND PRESERVED HER CHASTITY IN-
VIOLATE, BY THE MOST ARTFUL CONCEALMENT OF HER SEX.

WITH AN
### APPENDIX,
CONTAINING
CHARACTERISTIC TRAITS, BY DIFFERENT HANDS; HER
TASTE FOR ECONOMY, PRINCIPLES OF DOMESTIC EDUCA-
TION, &c.

*By a CITIZEN of MASSACHUSETTS.*

## D E D H A M :
PRINTED BY
### NATHANIEL AND BENJAMIN HEATON.
FOR THE *AUTHOR.*

M,DCC,XCVII.

TARRYTOWN, NEW YORK
REPRINTED
WILLIAM ABBATT
1916
Being Extra Number 47 of THE MAGAZINE OF HISTORY WITH NOTES AND QUERIES

# FEMALE REVIEW:

## OR,

## MEMOIRS

### OF AN

## AMERICAN YOUNG LADY

### CHAPTER I

A laconic History of Miss Sampson's extraction.—Local, and other situations of her parents.—Her endowments—natural temper and disposition.—Her propensities for learning.

DEBORAH SAMPSON was born in Plympton, a small village in the county of Plymouth in New England, December 17, 1760.[1] She is a regular descendant of the honorable family

[1] Her pedigree on the father's side is as follows: –

I. Abraham Sampson[1] came to Plymouth either in August, 1629, or in May of the following year. He was then a young man, and appears to have belonged to the English congregation at Leyden, in Holland, and to have come over with such members of that congregation as chose to remove to America after the death of their pastor, Rev. John Robinson. There can be no doubt that he was a brother of Henry Sampson, who came in the Mayflower, when a boy, in 1620. Abraham Sampson settled in Duxbury, where Henry also resided, and died there, at an advanced age, about the year 1690. He had four sons, who became heads of families,—Samuel[2], George[2], Abraham[2], Isaac.[2*]

II. Isaac Sampson[2], the youngest son, was born in Duxbury, in 1660. He was one of the first settlers of Plympton, a town originally a part of Plymouth, but incorporated as a separate municipality in 1707. He died in Plympton, September 3, 1726. His wife was Lydia Standish[3], daughter of Alexander Standish[2], and grand-daughter of Miles Standish[1], the military leader of the Pilgrims. The mother of Lydia Standish was Sarah Alden,[2] daughter of John Alden[1], that "hopeful young man," as Bradford calls him, who joined the Pilgrim company at Southampton, in August, 1620, and spent a long life in important services to the Plymouth Colony, dying, in 1687, at the age of eighty-eight.

*This expression Isaac[2], denotes that Isaac[2] was of the second generation, counting from and including the first American ancestor.

of William Bradford,[2] a native of England, a man of excellent natural endowments, upon which, he made great improvement by
learning.   He emigrated to America whilst young; where he was
for many years alternately, elected Governor of the Colony of
Plymouth.   In this department he presided with wisdom and punc-
tuality, and to the unanimous satisfaction of the people under his
charge.   He married an American lady of distinction, by whom he
had considerable issue.   As he lived beloved and reverenced, he
died lamented by all, 1756.

Her grand-father, Elisha Bradford,[3] was a native of Plymouth

III.  Jonathan Sampson[3], the second son of Isaac Sampson[2] and of Lydia Standish[3], was
born in 1690, and lived in Plympton all his days.   Like his father and grandfather, he was a
tiller of the soil.   His wife was Joanna Lucas.   He died in Plympton, February 3, 1758, aged
68.   He had but one son, who arrived at mature years, named for himself, to wit:—
IV.  Jonathan Sampson[4], junior, who was born in Plympton, April 3, 1729.   He was by
his wife Deborah Bradford[4], the father of Deborah Sampson, the heroine of this story.—[See
Sampson Genealogy, in the "Giles Memorial," issued, in 1864, by the editor.]

2  William Bradford[1] was born at Austerfield, in Yorkshire, England, in 1588.   His father
and grandfather lived in the same place, and bore the same name.   About 1608, he went with
Mr. Robinson's congregation to Amsterdam, and in 1609 to Leyden.   He came to Plymouth in
the *Mayflower*, accompanied by his wife, whose maiden name was Dorothy May.   This lady,
however, never reached Plymouth, but was accidentally drowned, December 7, 1620, while the
*Mayflower* remained in the harbor of Provincetown.   His second wife, married August 14, 1623,
was the widow Alice Southworth, who had just arrived in the *Ann*.   After the death of Carver,
in April, 1621, Mr. Bradford was chosen Governor of the infant colony.   He was re-elected to
that office every year till 1657, except five years,—1633, '34, '36, '38, '44.   In those years he
was chosen Assistant.   For thirty-seven years, he was the foremost man in Plymouth Colony.
He was acquainted not only with the Dutch and French languages, but with the Latin, Greek,
and Hebrew,   For an unselfish public spirit, and a general nobleness of character, he has had
among men no superior.   At his death, which took place May 9, 1657 (not 1756, as stated in
the text), he was "lamented by all the colonies of New England, as a common blessing and
father to them all."   By his second wife, he was the father of William[2], who distinguished himself as a commander of the Plymouth forces in "Philip's War," and was several years Deputy
Governor of the colony; and of Joseph[2], who was born in 1630, and married Jael, daughter of
Rev. Peter Hobart, first minister of Hingham, in 1664.   Joseph Bradford[2] lived in Kingston,
then a part of Plymouth, on Jones River, half a mile from its mouth.

3  Elisha Bradford[3] was the son of Joseph Bradford[2], last mentioned, and grandson of the
Governor.   His first wife was Hannah Cole; his second, Bathsheba Le Broche, as in the text.
The Bradford Genealogy gives, as the date of the second marriage, September 7, 1718, which
must be correct, as the first child by this marriage was born in April, 1719.   His children were—
By first wife:—Hannah[4], who married Joshua Bradford[4], b. June 23, 1710, son of Israel Brad-

in New England. He possessed good abilities, and explored many sources that led him to literary distinction. As he was eminent in property, so piety, humanity and uprightness were the distinguishing characteristics of his life. He was married, September 7, 1719, to Bathsheba Le Broche, a French lady of elegant extraction and accomplishments. Her father was a native of Paris. He left a large issue; of which Miss Sampson's mother is one. But Mr. Bradford, for one of his benevolent offices, being bound for a ship and rich cargo belonging to a merchant of the same town, had the misfortune to lose the greater part of his interest. Thus deprived, at once, of what he had learned to prize by the industry and economy it cost him, it is natural to suppose it was no small discouragement to him, and that the face of things wore a different aspect around him: especially when we reflect, that the fulfilment of those principles, which exert themselves in acts of benevolence and affection towards all persons, depend, greatly, on wealth. Being at this time considerably advanced in years, this circumstance, together with the loss of his eldest son, preyed fast upon his constitution: And he did not long survive to mourn the loss of what seemed not in his power to remedy.

Miss Sampson's parents, though endowed with good abilities, cannot, in an eminent degree, be distinguished either by fortune or scientific acquisition. Her father was an only son, and heir to

ford[3] of Kingston, who was a son of Major William Bradford[2], and grandson of the Governor. Joshua Bradford[4] removed from Kingston to Meduncook, now Friendship, Maine, where, on May 27, 1756, both himself and wife were killed by a party of Indians, who carried their children to Canada, where they remained in captivity till the conquest of that province by the English, in 1759. They then returned to Meduncook. By second wife:—Hannah[4], b. April 10, 1719.* Joseph[4], b. December 17, 1721. Nehemiah[4], b. July 27, 1724. Laurana[4], b. March 26, 1726; married Elijah McFarland of Plympton. Mary[4], b. August 1, 1727. Elisha[4], b. October 6, 1729. Lois[4], b. January 30, 1731. Deborah[4], b. November 18, 1732; married Jonathan Sampson, jr.: she was the mother of Deborah Sampson. Alice[4], b. November 3, 1734; married—Waters of Sharon, Mass. Asenath[4], b. September 15, 1736. Carpenter[4], b. February 7, 1739. Abigail[4], b. June 20, 1741. Chloe[4], b. April 6, 1743.—]Bradford Genealogy, in *Gen. Reg.*, vol. iv., p. 48.

*Instances are not wanting in our early records of the giving of the same name to another child in the same family during the lifetime of the first.

no inconsiderable estate.   And if it be asked why her parents had
not a more liberal education? the answer may be a general objection:—Different persons are actuated by different objects of pursuit.   Some, it is evident, have leading propensities for the accumulation of lucrative gain: whilst others, who possess it, gladly
embrace the opportunity for their advancement in literature.

It was doubtless the intention of Mr. Bradford to have given
his children good education.   But whether the wreck in his fortune,
or whether his numerous progeny restrained the liberality of his
bestowments in this respect, I pretend not to affirm.   It is however more than probable, that her mother's, and perhaps her
father's, education, in some respects, was superior to that of the
commonalty

It is no dishonorable trait in the character of any in America
to be born farmers; even if they pursue the occupation through
life.   Their aim, however, must be to furnish themselves with the
requisites which will render them useful and happy, and those who
are round about them.   Had the latter of these blessings been conferred on Miss Sampson's father, he might, peradventure, have
surmounted difficulties, which it is thought, tended to make him
fickle and perhaps too loose in his morals.   He met with a sad disappointment in his father's estate, occasioned by the ill designs,
connivings and insinuations of a brother-in-law.[4]   Thus, he was
disinherited of a portion that belonged to him by hereditary right.
This circumstance, alone, made such impressions on his mind, that
instead of being fired with a just spirit of resentment and emulation to supply, by good application and economy, that of which he

4 His father, Jonathan Sampson, senior, died in 1758.   In the division of the estate, which
took place in 1759, a brother-in-law managed to deprive him (Deborah's father) of what he expected as his share of the property.   Whether the expectation were well founded or not, does
not appear.   For aught that appears on the Probate Records, the distribution was fair, though
it may have been otherwise.   The disappointment occurred only the year before Deborah's
birth, and seems to have made him desperate.   Mortified pride seems to have driven him from
home.   He appears to have fallen into habits of intemperance.   His wife was an estimable
woman.

had been unjustly deprived, he was led into opposite pursuits, which she laments, as being his greatest misfortune.

Such was her father's local situation after his marriage with her mother. She informs that she had but very little knowledge of her father during her juvenile years. Despairing of accumulating an interest by his domestic employments, his bent of mind led him to follow the seafaring business, which, as her mother informed her, he commenced before her birth. However great his prospects were, that fortune would prove more propitious to his prosperity and happiness upon the ocean than it had done on the land, he was effectually disappointed:—For after he had continued this fruitless employment some years, he took a voyage to some part of Europe, from whence he was not heard of for some years. At length, her mother was informed, he had perished in a shipwreck.

By this time his unsuccessful fortune, both by land and sea, had the tendency to break up his family. Her mother, however, by her industry and economical management, kept her family together as long as possible after her husband's supposed catastrophe. But she, meeting with sickness, and other providential misfor tunes, was obliged, at length, to disband her family and to scatter her children abroad.[5]

It may perhaps be remarked, that nothing uncommonly singular has attended Miss Sampson in the primeval stages of her life. Yet the inquisitive and curious mind, which is never tired in tracing the events and performances of the most distinguished characters, is wont to extend its researches still further, and to enquire where and how they have lived, and by what methods and gradations they arrived at the summit of their undertakings. I believe it is a truth to which we may generally assent, that most

5 There were five children, two sons and three daughters, viz.: Robert Shurtleff. Ephraim. Sylvia, who married, April 6, 1799, Jacob Cushman, b. February 29, 1747-8, son of Benjamin Cushman of Plympton.—See *Cushman Genealogy*. Deborah, b. December 17, 1760, the heroine of our story. The fifth child was a daughter, whose name is to us unknown.

illustrious characters originate, either from very low or very high birth and circumstances.—I therefore beg the reader's indulgence, whilst I trace the most singular circumstances and events that occurred to Miss Sampson during her juvenility; which may not be deemed wholly useless and unentertaining.

She was scarcely five years old, when the separation from her mother was occasioned by indigent circumstances.[6] The affectionate and prudent parent can best describe the emotions experienced by the mother and her daughter upon this occasion. The young Miss Sampson had already contracted an attachment to letters; and in many other respects promised fair to crown the instructions and assiduity of a parent, or patroness, with the most desirable success. And it was with pain her mother saw these flattering symptoms without being able to promote, or scarcely to encourage them by the fosterage of parental care and affection. Nor was the darkness of the scene dissipated, until a distant relation of her mother's, an elderly maiden by the name of Fuller, proffered to adopt her into her family, and take the charge of her education.[7]

This was a very honest and discreet lady. She shewed her young pupil many tokens of care and affection. But as Miss Sampson remarked—"As I was born to be unfortunate, my sun soon clouded." She had not continued in this agreeable situation scarcely three years, before her benefactress was seized with a violent malady, which in a few days proved fatal.

6 Notwithstanding the "indigent circumstances" out of which our heroine emerged, it should be borne in mind that some of the best blood of the Old Colony flowed in her veins. A descendant of John Alden, of Miles Standish, of Peter Hobart, and of William Bradford, and a cousin-german of Captain Simeon Samson, one of the distinguished naval commanders of the Revolution,—there was much in her family connections to gratify an honest pride.

7 Thus was Deborah, in the tender period of childhood, when the heart is most open to impressions, and when it most needs the counsels and the restraints of parental love, virtually bereft of both her parents. The loss she now sustained could never be repaired. She had already exhibited indications of talent, and a thirst for knowledge. She had, under the tuition of her mother, begun to read. Her perceptions were quick, her imagination lively, her affections warm. Could her talents have been developed by proper culture, she might have adorned an elevated position in society.

Although she was, at that time, not more than eight years old, she was much affected with the loss of her patroness.—She deemed it almost irreparable:—considered herself without a home, or scarcely a friend to procure her one. But this scene was too distressing to last long. Her mother, hearing of her circumstances, endeavored to obtain a suitable place for her, till she should come of age. She was put into one Mrs. Thacher's family in Middleborough, where she continued about two years.[8] This lady took particular care to gratify her favorite propensity for reading, &c., but as she was of a slender constitution, her mother removed her to Mr. Jeremiah Thomas's, of the same town.[9]

Is it indeed, sadly true that nature, our common source of be-

8 It has been supposed, and not without reason, that this lady was the widow of Rev. Peter Thacher, the third minister of Middleborough. Mr. Thacher was born in Milton, October 6, 1688, and was son of Rev. Peter Thacher of that place, and grandson of Rev. Thomas Thacher, first minister of the Old South Church in Boston. He was pastor of the Church in Middleborough from 1709 till his death, in 1744, in the 56th year of his age. If the supposition just mentioned be correct, Mrs. Thacher must have been, at the time when Deborah was in her family, more than eighty years of age, as she died in 1771, aged 84. In this case, services may have been required which a child ten years old was not able to perform. Plympton has Middleborough on the south-west, joining it.

9 The *History of the First Church in Middleborough*, printed about twelve years since, contains a list of all who have been members of that church from its organization, in 1695, to 1853. This list appears to have been compiled with uncommon care. It contains the name of only one Jeremiah Thomas; and he died in 1736, ae.77. The individual intended in the text must have been Benjamin Thomas, who was chosen deacon in 1776, and died January 18, 1800, ae. 78. In the MS. memoir of Deborah Sampson, he is called "Deacon Thomas," without any mention of his baptismal name, which Deborah had evidently forgotten. The following facts are related of him in the *History of the First Church*, already mentioned: "Deacon Thomas, though not of a cultivated mind in other respects, was well versed in the Scriptures, of inflexible virtue, of sound and clear orthodoxy, and conscientious in the performance of known duty; holding on upon the old landmarks, and refusing to let them go. In 1782, he was a representative in the Legislature, and, in 1788, a member of the Convention which adopted the Federal Constitution. A bill was under discussion for repealing the law of primogeniture. The deacon expressed his doubts on the matter, because the Scriptures showed special favors to the first born. A Boston gentleman said that 'the deacon mistook the Scriptures; for they said that Jacob, though the younger brother, inherited the birthright.' The deacon replied, 'The gentleman had forgotten to tell us how he obtained it,—how Esau sold his birthright for a mess of pottage, and how Jacob deceived his father, pretending to be Esau, and how his mother helped on the deception,—he had forgotten all that!' The laugh, which was at first against the deacon, was now turned against the gentleman from Boston." The deacon was more than a match for him.

ing, is unequal in her intellectual bestowments on the human species? If not, the apparent difference must be in the manner in which they are exhibited.  This I am inclined to believe: and the greatest remedy is education.  Hence the shrewd saying—"Learning keeps him out of fire and water."—An excellent stimulation for every one.  Logicians, I trust, will allow me to form an estimation of Miss Sampson's endowments, even before she had reached her teens.  This I do, without a design to flatter her into vain conceits of herself, or to wheedle any one of the human species into her favor, or esteem of the writer.  It is a just tribute of respect due to the illustrious poor.

Certain it is that she early discovered, at least to every judicious observer, tokens of a fertile genius and an aspiring mind: a mind quick of perception and of strong penetration.  And if it be allowable to judge of things past by their present aspect, I hesitate not to announce that her primeval temper was uniform and tranquil.  Though destitute of many advantages of education, she happened to fix on many genuine principles.  She may be noted for a natural sweetness and pliability of temper—a ready wit, which only needed refinement—a ready conformity to a parent's, or patroness' injunctions—a native modesty and softness in expression and deportment, and passions naturally formed for philanthropy and commiseration.

A further enumeration might give occasion for a new apology.  Nor have I a right to describe her abilities in proportion to the improvements she has since made.  I might fall into gross errors.  Nature might complain of injustice for making a wrong estimate of her bounties.  And it is a truth, too often to be lamented, that she oftener complains of uncultivated talents, than for not giving any for cultivation.  Our endowments, of course, must be equal, if not superior to our improvements.  Should the contrary be urged, those principles which have dictated her exertions, might lose a part of their energetic influence; in which she still delights.  Had she shared greater advantages in education, she might have much exceeded the proficiency in erudition, but scarcely the singularity of character, which she has since attained.

It was a circumstance peculiarly unhappy with Miss Sampson, during her minority, that she found less opportunities than inclinations for learning. The instances I shall adduce to corroborate this assertion, will be comprised in the next chapter;—where the reader will find a general sketch of her education during this period.

I shall only add, that many of our humble peasantry in America would have thanked fortune, if this evil had been confined to her. It is not so great a wonder, as it is a lamentable truth, which observation in many families may evince, that they have amassed together a greater bulk of riches than of useful science; whilst perhaps, the man who never could obtain a mediocrity of wealth, only needed it to vie with them in every thing useful and ornamental. Thus the most fertile genius, like that of soil, which for want of proper cultivation is overrun with noxious weeds, becomes corrupted by neglect and vicious habit: and the inherent beauties that might have eclipsed a more than ordinary show, lie dormant.

Where then, could the Guardians of science have been secreted! or had they not taken an universal charge of this growing empire!—Instances of this kind, however, are more rarely met with than formerly. And this error will always find the best apology in the population of new countries, where the means for subsistence unavoidably demand the most attention. But affluence, without being regulated by refined education, cloys the sight of the beholder; and the possessors are unqualified for duty. The minds of people are now roused by the introduction of new scenes and objects. And it is here to be repeated, to the honor of the citizens of New England, and the United States in general, that they are, with success, endeavoring to counterbalance this once prevailing evil; at least they would make an equilibrium between their wealth and literature.

Let not, therefore, any who ha**v**e talents for improvement, despair of success in any situation.   Though a Franklin has become extinct, a Washington survives.   Our native land smiles under the fostering hand of industry and economy.   It will still produce our men of government, our guardians of science, and our encouragers and promoters of virtue.

CHAPTER II

Miss Sampson's propensities for learning, and the obstacles she met with in it, contrasted. —View of her education during her juvenility—in which time, she contracts a taste for the study of nature or natural philosophy; which teaches her regular ideas of Deity—the necessity of morality and decorum in her pursuits.

WE are now to view Miss Sampson advancing into the bloom and vigor of youth.   In this season comes on the trial of virtue and of the permanency of that foundation, upon which improvements have begun.   The passions having assumed greater degrees of vigor, and still susceptible of quick and delicate impressions from their natural attachment to the sexes, and other alluring objects of pursuit, it becomes accountable that so many of both sexes, especially those deprived of genuine education, fail of that uniform course of improvement in knowledge and virtue which is the only barrier against vice and folly, and our surest guidance through life.   If she be found, at this age, persevering in these duties and surmounting the principal allurements to indecorum and vice, I need not hesitate to announce her a singular paradigm for many in better circumstances and in higher life.

From the time she went to live in Mr. Thomas's family,[10] till

10  Deborah lived in the family of Deacon Thomas from the age of ten to that of eighteen. His house was in a retired spot, about two miles east of the central village of Middleborough Four Corners.   It was a substantial building, the timbers and roof-boards being made of white-oak.   Here Deborah was well clad, and her physical wants were well supplied.   The deacon had a good farm, and he and his family were good livers.   Deborah's health became confirmed, and she acquired a bodily vigor which fitted her to encounter the hardships of subsequent years.   She became acquainted with almost all kinds of manual labor proper to her sex.

186

she was eighteen, it may be said she lived in common with other youth of her own sex; except in two very important respects:— She had stronger propensities for improvement, and less opportunities to acquire it. Industry and economy—excellent virtues! being hereditary in this family, she was of course inured to them. And as their children were numerous, and chiefly of the masculine sex, it is not improbable that her athletic exercises were more intense on that account. As they appeared more eager in the amassing of fortune than of scientific acquisition, she was obliged to check the bud, which had already begun to expand, and to yield the palm of the fulfilment of her duty to her superintendents in the manner they deemed best, to the sacrifice of her most endearing propensities But painful was the thought that she must suffer the bolt to be turned upon this, her favorite pursuit. Wounding was the sight of others going to school, when she could not, because she could not be spared. Her reflections were singular, considering her age, when contrasting her privileges with those of other children, who had parents to take the charge of their education. It was a circumstance effectually mortifying to her, that she could not hold familiarity, even with the children of the family, on their school topics. But the ambition that agitated her mind made her wont to believe her lot as good as that of orphans in general.

Happy it was for her, at this age, that neither mortification nor prohibition impeded her inherent propensity for learning. This instead of being weakened, was strengthened by time; though she had not devised any effectual method to gratify it. She had often heard—that a forward and promising youth is short lived. But she did not believe it. And in this respect her longevity was rested

She learned to spin and weave, accomplishments which were then thought indispensable to a young woman. She could also, when occasion required, harness the family horse, and ride him to plough, or to the village on errands. She was not only familiar with the work of the dairy, but when a shower was coming up could rake hay, and help to stow it away in the barn. She was, moreover, a tolerable mechanic. If she wanted a basket, a milking-stool, or a sled, she could make it. Indeed, she acquired the habit of adapting herself to existing circumstances, whatever they might be.

on as good safety, as was that of the wisest man: Nor have I the
least inclination to censure either. The preceptor knows it is a
task to kindle sparks of emulation in most children; and reason informs him, when they are naturally kindled, it is an injurious en-
gine that extinguishes the flame

It is the pride of some undisciplined, tyrannical tempers to
triumph over supposed ignorance, distress and poverty. In this
our better-deserving orphan found a source of mortification.[11] But
magnanimity and hope—ever soothing companions! elevated her
above despair. The ideas of being rivalled by her mates in learning
and decorum, guarded their proper receptacle, and prompted the
establishment of the following maxims:—Never neglect the least
circumstance that may be made conducive to improvement: Opportunity is a precious companion; which is too often sadly verified
by the fool's companions, folly and procrastination—thieves that
rob the world of its treasure.

Her method was to listen to every one she heard read and
speak with propriety. And when she could, without intrusion,
catch the formation of a letter from a penman, she gladly embraced
it. She used to obtain what school books and copies she could
from the children of the family, as models for her imitation. Her
leisure interims were appropriated to these talks with as little reluctance as common children went to play.

Availing herself of such methods with unremitted ardor, together with promiscuous opportunities at school, she at length
found herself mistress of pronunciation and sentences to such a degree, that she was able to read, with propriety, in almost any book

11 There is no reason to suppose that anything of this sort was true of Deacon Thomas or
any of his family. He was a most worthy man, careful and conscientious in all things; but,
like most of the New England farmers of that age, he could not comprehend the value of learning, except as it contributed to immediate practical results. Deborah was bound to him till
the age of eighteen; and he considered himself entitled to her services whenever they were
wanted. She attended school a part of the time; and, when out of school, she induced the children of the family to teach her. The scanty opportunities allowed, she improved to the utmost.

in her language. The like application, in process of time qualified her to write a legible hand. As soon as she could write, she voluntarily kept a journal of common occurrences; an employment not unworthy the humblest peasant, or the most renowned sage.[12]

The anxiety and aspirations of her mind after knowledge at length became more notorious to many, who made learning their element. As catechetical tuition, in some respects, was more in use thirty years ago than now, she committed to memory, at an early age, the Catechism by the Assembly of Divines, and could recite a prolix proof of it verbatim.[13] By this she secured the esteem and approbation of her village curate;[14] which he expressed by many flattering expressions, and a donation of a few books. And to mention the epistolary correspondence, which she commenced at the age of twelve, with a young lady of polite accomplishments who had not only offered to supply her with paper, but with whatever instructions she could, would be reminding her of a debt which she could only repay by her gratitude for such obliging condescention. The correspondence was of much utility to her in her future employments.

Thus, so much genius and taste were not always to remain sequestered, like a pearl in the bowels of the deep, or in an inaccessible place. Nor must I insinuate that she was here deprived of many other principal advantages of education. She fared well

12 She kept this journal on the singular plan of recording her good deeds on the first, third, fifth, &c., pages, and her bad deeds on the opposite pages. As might be expected, the opposite pages were soonest filled.

13 The Catechism was doubtless committed to memory by all the young members of the family. This was a family of the good old Puritan stamp, exact in the observance of the Sabbath, regular attendants on public worship, punctual in their daily devotions. The parents disapproved, and indeed prohibited to those under their care, all gay and frivolous amusements; and taught them, both by precept and example, the strictest lessons of morality and virtue. But so much serious religion was irksome to the buoyant spirit of Deborah; and she contracted a disrelish for it which remained in after-life.

14 "Her village curate"—strange expresson!—was Rev. Sylvanus Conant. He was pastor of the First Church in Middleborough from March 28, 1745, till his death, December 8, 1777.

for food and raiment; and that, she reflected, was better than could
be said of many of her surrounding companions. It is with respect and gratitude she speaks of her superintendents on many
other accounts. She has often said with emotion that the most
mortifying punishment she ever received from her master, was—
"You are always hammering upon some book—I wish you would-
n't spend so much time in scribbling over paper." Had he been
possessed of Miss Hannah More's beautiful satire, he might, more
politely, have recited the same ideas:

> "I wish she'd leave her books, and mend her clothes:
> I thank my stars, I know no verse from prose."

They not only carefully habituated her to industry and domestic
economy in general, but from them, her mistress in particular, she
experienced lessons of morality and virtue, which she thinks could
not have failed to have been beneficial to any one whose heart had
not been too much tipped with adamantine hardness, or whose
faculties had not been totally wrapped in inattention. Indeed,
the laborious exercises to which she was accustomed during her
stay in this family, may be considered of real service to her. They
added strength and permanency to her naturally good constitution; kept the mind awake to improvements (for the mind will
doze, when indolence seizes the body), and thus prepared her to
endure the greater hardships which were to characterize her future
life.

It is with peculiar pleasure I here find occasion to speak of
Miss Sampson's taste for the study of Nature, or Natural Philosophy. More agreeable still would be my talk, had she enjoyed
opportunities, that her proficiency in it might have been equal to
her relish for it.

That Philosophy should ever have been treated with indifference, much less with intentional neglect, is an idea that affords
singular astonishment to every rational mind. The philosopher
has been considered as—not a man of this world; as an unsocial and

unfit companion, and wanting in the general duties of life.* Such ideas must have been the result of a very erroneous acceptation of the word, or of a mind not a little tinctured with prejudice. I have always conceived that philosophy is a scientific sphere, in which we are enjoined to act by nature, reason and religion; which serve as a directory, or auxiliaries to accelerate us in it. The philosopher, then, instead of being rendered a useless object in society, and wanting in the general duties of life, is the person most eminently qualified for a useful member of society, the most agreeably calculated for an intercourse and union with the sexes, best acquainted with the social and enjoined duties of life; and is thus preparing himself for a more refined being in futurity.

It must then have been merely from the abstruseness, which many people have falsely imagined attends this most plain and useful of all sciences, that they have been deterred from the pursuit of it. But however reprobated and useless the study of philosophy may have been deemed for the man of sense, and much more dangerous for the other sex, it is certain that it is now emerging from an obsolete state to that of a fashionable and reputable employment. Ignorance in it being now the thing mostly to be dreaded. And many of both sexes are not ashamed of having the appellation conferred on them in any situation in life.

I learn from Miss Sampson's diurnals, and from the credibility of others, that she early discovered a taste for the contemplation of the objects and appearances exhibited in creation. She was notorious for her frequent interrogatories relative to their nature, use and end. Nor is this, in a degree, unnatural for children in general. Natural Creation is a source that first excites the notice and attention of all. I have myself observed even infants, after long confinement, appear reanimated and filled with admiration on being again brought into the refulgence of the Sun or Moon, the

I here particularly allude to a small performance, which contains, among these, many excellent moral maxims. It was written by a female, and entitled—"The Whole Duty of Woman."

spangled appearance of the stars, the enamelled mead, the aspiring grove, or a single floweret. Thus they make it a voluntary act to enquire into their origin, use and end. Whereas it often happens, that the same child, by reason of some nursed, ill habit of temper, will brook no controul by the best moral precept or example, except it be from the dread of corporeal punishment.— This, therefore, should rouze the attention of parents. As the first dawning of reason in their children displays itself in this way, they should make it their peculiar care to assist and encourage it in every respect. Nature, indeed, may be considered as a general monitor and instructor. But it is from experience and practical experiments that we are facilitated in the acquisition of knowledge.

Here taste for the cultivation of plants and vegetable productions in general, appears to have been somewhat conspicuous in her early years. And she has intimated an idea of this kind, which, from its justness, and the delicate effects it has on many of the softer passions, induces me to notice it. It has been a source of astonishment and mortification to her that so many of her own, as well as of the other sex, can dwell with rapture on a romantic scene of love, a piece of painting or sculpture, and, perhaps, upon things of more trivial importance; and yet can walk in the stately and venerable grove, can gaze upon the beautifully variegated landscape, can look with indifference upon the rose and tulip, or can tread on a bank of violets and primroses, without appearing to be affected with any peculiar sensations and emotions. This certainly proceeds from a wrong bias of the mind in its fixing on its first objects of pursuit. And parents cannot be too careful in the prevention of such errors, when they are forming the minds of their offspring for the courses which are to affect the passions, and give sway to the behavior during life.

I know not whether it was from her mental application to books, instructions from public or private preceptors, or from her own observations on nature, that she acquired the most knowledge of philosophy and astronomy. Perhaps it was from some advantage. of the whole. I am however authorized to say, both from her infant memorandums and verbal communications, that she did obtain, during her juvenility, many just ideas respecting them. She has assured me the questions she used to ask, relative to the rising and setting of the Sun, Moon, &c., never ceased agitating her mind till she had formed proper ideas of the spherical figure of the Earth, and of its diurnal and annual revolutions. In this manner, she acquired a smattering of the Solar System. But she has no wish even now, for having the appellation philosopher or astronomer, conferred on her. But my readers may conclude it is merely on account of her fancied ignorance of those sublime sciences.

She frequently made it her custom to rise in the morning before twilight. During the Spring, Summer and Autumn, it seems, she was peculiarly attached to rural speculation. And, as though she had been a Shepherdess, she was frequently seen in some adjacent field, when the radiant orb of day first gleamed on the hill tops to cheer and animate vegetable nature with his prolific and penetrating rays.

The studious and contemplative mind can best interpret her motive in this, and the utility of it. To those who have seldom or never enjoyed the delicious repasts of this tranquil hour, it may be said—the mind, like the body, having rested from the toils and bustle of the day, awakes in a state of sereneness the best calculated for contemplation, for the reception and impression of ideas, which this season, above all others, seems capable of affording. The physician may also inform, that early rising is a cordial and preservative of health. It creates a lively carnation on the cheek, adds vigor and activity to the limbs and senses, which no one wishes to exchange for the languishing constitution, the pallid countenance, and mind staggering with the weight of an inactive body, of him who takes too much repose on his downy pillow.

The dawning of day—when the sun is dissipating the darkness, all nature assuming reanimation, each tribe of instinct hastening to its respective occupation, and man, who had been confined in morbid inactivity, reassuming strength and cheerfulness—is emblematic of Creation rising out of its original chaos or non-existence.   Surely then, this scene cannot fail of filling the philosophic mind with just and sublime ideas, and with the purest love and gratitude to that Being, who caused them to exist and who still regulates and superintends the whole.

Miss Sampson has repeatedly said, that her mind was never more effectually impressed with the power, wisdom and beneficence of Deity than in the contemplation of his Creation.   It affords ideas the most familiar and dignified, and lessons the most striking, captivating and beautifully sublime.

The Earth, which is computed to be 25,038 English miles in circumference, and to contain about 199,512,595 square miles of surface, is indeed a large body.*   The thoughts of its construction, of its convenient situations for its innumerable species of inhabitants, and of the abundance of good it affords them, are sufficient to warm the human breast with all that is tender and benevolent.

But our creative faculties in their researches are not limited to this globe.   The sight is attracted into boundless ether, to roam amongst the other revolutionary orbs and spangled situations of the fixed stars.†   In this nature is our prompter, and reason our guide. Here we are led to believe, without doubt, that such orbs as are visible to the eye, occupy immensity.   And the probability is that millions, yea, an infinite number of such bodies are peopled by inhabitants not dissimilar to our own.   And when we further consider the immense distance there is between each of these planets, stars or suns, and the certainty of the regularity and mutual harmony that forever subsists between them, although they are per-

*See Esq. Guthrie's and Dr. Morse's Geographies.

†Considered by modern philosophers and astronomers, as suns.

petually whirling with the most inconceivable veloicty; what august
and amazing conceptions do we have of that Being who has fabricated their existence! Surely then the mind that is not lost to all
sense of rectitude and decorum, must be filled with ideas the most
dignified, with sentiments and passions the most refined, and with
gratitude the most abundant and sincere.

As Miss Sampson had a natural attachment to the study of
creation, it would have been unnatural, and even criminal, to have
been negligent in forming an acquaintance with her own nature
—with its important use and end. Everything in nature, as well
as in reason, enjoins this as a duty. The uniformity everywhere
observable in creation, doubtless was influential and subservient
to the regulation of her moral and civil life. This may excite an
idea of novelty with those who do not studiously attend the lec-
tures of Nature. But had we no other directory by which we could
regulate our lives and conduct, and were it not possible to deviate
from this, there would be less danger of the confusion so often visible among mankind, of immorality, and of the sword, which is even
now deluging such a part of the world in blood.

From an habitual course of speculations like these, she may
be said to have been reasonably impressed with the following
theoretical conclusions drawn from them: That human nature is
born in imperfection; the great business of which is refinement, and
constant endeavors of approximation to perfection and happiness;
—That ignorance and the general train of evils are the natural offspring of inattention, and that all tend to the degradation of our
nature;—And that diligent application is the great requisite for
improvement; which only can dignify and exalt our nature and our
character.

These traits, I venture to affirm, are some of the primeval
exertions of those endowments, which are so peculiarly characteristic of our rectitude and worth. They are leading principles of

life. I take the liberty to call them spontaneous; because they are more or less natural to every one.

Impelled by desires to promote virtue and decorum, as well as by justice, I here mention one more trait of her juvenility: and I could wish it might not distinguish her from others at this day. During this season, it may be said, she was generally a stranger and showed an aversion to all irregular and untimely diversions. Nor is she more deserving a panegyric on this account than her superintendents. She despised revelry, gossipping, detraction and orgies, not because she was originally any better than others, but because they were unfashionable in her neighborhood;—and especially, because her master and mistress not only disapproved, but prohibited them. This theory is certainly good, however bad her practice hereafter may appear. Their practice, rather than their name should be struck out of time.

Perhaps I make a greater distinction than many do between what is called the universal ruin of nature, and that occasioned by wrong education. We call nature corrupt: instead of which, we may say corporeal substance. The immortal part of man is pure; and it is the pride of genuine nature to keep it so. It is embarrassed many times by a vicious body: but it will remain uncontaminated, though the body tumbles into dissolution.

Custom bears great sway: even the palate may be made to relish any diet by custom. But this argues not that anything can be received by the stomach without danger. We are the pilots of our children; and on us they depend for safety. They learn by imitation, as well as by precept. And I have either read, heard or thought (no matter which) that children will always be gazing on the signs their parents have lettered.—We wish for reformation in youth; but let age be careful to lay the foundation stone.

It is not presumed that Miss Sampson was at this age, without particular blemishes and foibles. Like others destitute of principal advantages of education, she was doubtless culpable for the misimprovement of much time and many talents. Whilst her superintendents may corroborate this, they are ready to do her the justice of saying, that she was a lover of order in their family—punctual in the fulfilment of her duty to them, and assiduous to heighten their regard for her. And that her obligations of this nature did not terminate here, many of her cotemporaries, I dare say, can testify. Studious to increase a reciprocity of affection with her relations and surrounding companions, she was successful. To behave with temperance to strangers, is what she deemed a step of prudence: But to show an indifference, or actually to disoblige a friend or companion, could only be repaid by redoubled attention to restore them to her favor, and by acknowledged gratitude for their lenity.

On the whole, we must look upon her endowments, in general, during her juvenility, as the statuary may look upon his marble in the quarry; or as any one may look upon a rich piece of painting or sculpture, which combines uniformity with profusion; yet where the hand of the artist has not discovered every latent beauty, nor added a finishing polish to those that are apparent.

CHAPTER III

Analysis of Miss Sampson's thoughts on the rise and progress of the American War, with a concise account of the Lexington and Breed's Hill engagements—including a remarkable dream.

THE motives that led to hostilities between North America and Great Britain, and the period that terminated our relation to and dependence on that nation are events the most singular and important we have ever known:—singular, because in their very nature, they were unnatural;—important, because on them depended the future welfare and lustre of America.

197

The operations of these affairs, both before and after the first engagement at Lexington, are well known to have affected the minds, even of both sexes, throughout the Colonies, with sensations and emotions different from whatever they had before experienced. Our progenitors had suffered almost every hardship in their first settlement of this country, and much bloodshed by the Aborigines. But these are events that naturally attend the population of new countries; and consequently, naturally anticipated. But when our property, which our ancestors had honestly acquired, was invaded; when our inherent rights were either prohibited or infringed, an alarm was universally given; and our minds were effectually awakened to the keenest sense of the injuries, and naturally remained in distress, till we became exempt from their jurisdiction.

Perhaps the public may not be surprised that events, so interesting and important, should arrest the attention of any one. But when either of the sexes reverses its common sphere of action, our curiosity is excited to know the cause and event. The field of war is a department peculiarly assigned to the hero. It may therefore appear somewhat curious, if not interesting to many, when they are informed that this uncommonly arrested the attention of a Young Female of low birth and station. Miss Sampson is the one who not only listened to the least information relative to the rise and progress of the late American War; but her thoughts were, at times, engrossed with it. I will analyze them, as I find them sketched in her credentials, or as I learn them from credible authorities.

Before the blockade of Boston, March 5th, 1775, by the British, the Colonies had been thrown into great confusion and distress by repeated acts of oppression by the British, that produced riots which, in Boston, were carried to the greatest extremities. It was not till this time that Miss Sampson obtained information of the arrival of the King's troops, and of the spirited opposition maintained by the Americans. She justly learned that it was the Acts of the British Parliament to raise a revenue,* without her consent, that gave rise to these cruel and unjust measures.[15] Had she possessed information and experience on the subject, like many others, she would doubtless, like them, have seen the impropriety that England should have an unlimited controul over us, who are separated from her by the vast Atlantic, at least, three thousand miles.

But so it was.  From the first established settlement in North America, to the Declaration of our Independence, we acknowledged the sovereignty of the British Government and thus continued tributary to her laws.  And as though it had not been enough that she had driven many of our ancestors from their native clime, by the intolerant and unrelenting spirit of her religious persecution, to seek a new world, and to suffer the distress naturally consequent —they insisted still, that our property, our conduct and even our lives must be under their absolute controul.  Thus, we remained subject to the caprice of one, the influential chicanery of a second, and the arbitrary decision of the majority.  And it is not my prerogative to say we should not have remained loyal subjects of the Crown, to this day, had not our affections been alienated by the administration of laws, in their nature unjust, and calculated to injure none but those the least deserving of injury.

Perhaps there is no period in our lives in which the principles of humanity and benevolence can better take root, than in that of the juvenile age.  And it has been a rare instance, that the sit uation of any nation has been so effectually calculated to bring these to the act of experiment, as ours was at the juncture of our revolution.  The distressed situation of the inhabitants of Massachusetts, and particularly of those in the metropolis, after the

*In America.

15 There was no "blockade of Boston, March 5, 1775," aside from the closing of the port, under the "Boston Port Bill," which went into effect June 1, 1774.  Several British regiments were stationed in Boston from the middle of June, 1774.  "Without her consent!"  Without whose consent?

passing of the Port Bill, can never be remembered without starting the tear of humanity, and exciting the indignation of the world.

Miss Sampson, though not an eye witness of this distress, was not insensible of it. She learned that the inhabitants of Boston were confined by an unprovoked enemy; that they were not only upon the point of perishing for want of sustenance, but that many had been actually massacred, their public and private buildings of elegance shamefully defaced, or quite demolished; and that many of her own sex were either ravished, or deluded to the sacrifice of their chastity, which she had been taught to revere even as dear as life itself.

These thoughts filled her mind with sensations to which she had hitherto been unaccustomed—with a kind of enthusiasm which strengthened and increased with the progression of the war; and which, peradventure, fixed her mind in a situation from which she afterwards found it impossible to be extricated, until the accomplishment of the object after which it aspired.

During her residence in Mr. Thomas's family, they granted her many domestic privileges;—such as the use of a number of fowls, sheep, &c., upon condition, that she would appropriate the profit from them to the attainment of objects useful and ornamental. This was an effectual method to inure her to method and a proper use of money. She applied herself to the business with diligence and success. And at this time she had accumulated a small stock, which was appropriated, agreeably to her notion, perfectly coincident to the injunction. The poor people of Boston were reduced to the piteous necessity of asking charity, or contribution from the country inhabitants. This was no sooner known to her than she experienced an anxiety, that could brook no controul, until she had an opportunity of casting in her mite: Upon which she sincerely congratulated herself, not upon the principle that any one owed her any more gratitude; but upon the consciousness of having endeavoured to relieve the innocent and distressed.

Though I am as much disinclined to have faith in common dreams as in any invented fable, or to spend time in reciting their ominous interpretations, yet as they proceed from that immortal part of man, which no one ought to slight, they may sometimes be of use. I cannot help noticing in this place, a phenomenon presented to the mind of Miss Sampson during her nocturnal repose, April 15, 1775, in the fifteenth year of her age, and but four days before the battle at Lexington. I insert the principal part of it in her own language, and some of the latter part, verbatim.[16]

"As I slept, I thought, as the Sun was declining beneath our hemisphere, an unusual softness and sereneness of weather invited me abroad to perambulate the Works of Nature. I gladly embraced the opportunity; and with eager steps and pensive mind quickly found myself environed in the adjacent fields, which were decorated with the greatest profusion of delights. The gentle ascending ground on one side, upon which were grazing numerous kinds of herds; the pleasant and fertile valley and meadow, through which meandered small rivulets on the other; the aspiring and venerable grove, either before or behind me; the zephyrs, which were gently fanning the boughs, and the sweet caroling of the birds in the branches; the husbandmen, intent upon their honorable and most useful employment, agriculture; the earth, then cloathed with vegetation, which already filled the air with ravishing odours;—all conspired to fill my mind with sensations hitherto unknown, and to direct it to a realization of the Author of their being whose power, wisdom and goodness are, as they manifest, as infinite as they are perpetual.

Studious in contemplating the objects that surrounded me, I

16 In the MS. memoir of Deborah Sampson, she is represented as having had this dream on three successive nights, the last of which immediately preceded the "Lexington Alarm." *Credat Judaeus Apella, non ego.* In that memoir, the dream is told with much enlargement, and in extremely high-flown language. It is there represented as a prophecy of the American Revolution. Pretty well for a girl of fourteen! It is difficult to believe that this dream ever had any existence, save in the brain of Herman Mann. It is a pity to spoil with it so much white paper.

should have been barbarous, and perhaps have deprived myself of advantages which I never might again possess, had I abruptly quitted my ramble. I prolonged it till I found myself advanced upon a lofty eminence that overlooked a far more extensive and beautiful prospect, both of the ocean and continent.

Having reached the summit, I sat down to indulge such thoughts as the scene seemed altogether capable of inspiring.— How much, thought I, is it to be regretted that I am not always filled with the same sensations, with such sublime ideas of Creation, and of that Being who has caused it to exist! Indeed, I fancied I could joyfully have spent my life in researches for knowlledge in this delightsome way.

But how great was my astonishment and horror at the reversion of the scene! An unusual appearance, different from whatever my eyes beheld, or imagination suggested, was at once cast on everything that surrounded me. The sky, which before was so pleasant and serene, suddenly lowered, and became instantaneously veiled with blackness. Though not altogether like a common tempest, incessant lightning and tremendous peals of thunder seemed to lacerate the very vaults of nature. The ambrosial sweets of vegetation were exchanged for the nauseous stenches of sulphur and other once condensed bodies, that seemed to float in ether.

Happening at this instant to cast my eyes upon the liquid element, new amazement was added to the scene. Its surface, which before was unruffled, was now properly convulsed, and seemed piled in mountains to the sky. The ships that before were either anchored, or riding with tranquillity to their harbors, at once dismasted, dashing against rocks and one another, or floundering amidst the surges. The industrious farmers, many of whom were visited by their consorts in their rural occupations, seemed dispersed, and flying for refuge to the nearest place of safety.

And the birds and bestial tribes seemed at a loss where to go being, in as great confusion as the elements.

Filled with astonishment at this distraction of the elements, without any fixed precaution what method to take for safety; on the one side the earth, a volcano which shook with the perpetual roar of thunder, and on the other side the liquid element foaming to the clouds—my reason seemed entirely to forsake me, on beholding the most hideous serpent roll itself from the ocean. He advanced, and seemed to threaten carnage and destruction wherever he went. At length he approached me, with a velocity which I expected would instantly have cost me my life. I happened to be directed homeward; but looking back and perceiving the streets, through which he passed, drenched in blood, I fell into a swoon. In this condition, I know not how long I remained. At length I found myself (as I really was) in my own apartment; where I hoped not to be again shocked with the terrific and impending destruction of the elements or monster.

But to my repeated grief and amazement, I beheld the door of the apartment open of itself; and the serpent, in a more frightful form and venomous in looks, reappeared. He was of immense bigness; his mouth opened wide, and teeth of great length. His tongue appeared to have a sharp sting in the end. He entered the room, but it was not of sufficient dimensions for his length. As he advanced towards my bedside, his head raised, as nearly as I conjectured, about five or six feet, his eyes resembled balls of fire. I was frightened beyond description. I thought I covered my head and tried to call for assistance, but could make no noise.

At length, I heard a voice saying, "Arise, stand on your feet, gird yourself and prepare to encounter your enemy."—This seemed impossible, as I had no weapon of defence. I rose up, stood upon the bed; but before I had time to dress the serpent approached, and seemed resolved to swallow me whole. I thought I called on

God for assistance in these distressing moments: And at that instant, I beheld, at my feet a bludgeon, which I readily took into my hand, and immediately had a severe combat with the enemy. He retreated towards the door from whence he first entered. I pursued him closely and perceived, as he lowered his head, he attempted to strike me with his tail. His tail resembled that of a fish, more than that of a serpent. It was divided into several parts, and on each branch there were capital letters of yellow gilt. I pursued him after he left the apartment, several rods, striking him every opportunity; till at length I dislocated every joint, which fell in pieces to the ground: But the pieces reunited, though not in the form of a serpent, but in that of an Ox. He came at me a second time, roaring and trying to gore me with his horns. But I renewed the attack with such resolution, and beat him in such a manner, that he fell again in pieces to the ground. I ran to gather them; but on survey found them nothing but a jelly.— And I immediately awoke."

This very singular Dream had an uncommon effect on her mind, and seemed to presage some great event. The novelty and momentous ideas it inspired, induced her to record it; but she kept it secreted from others. At that time she attempted no particular interpretation of it.

Although the nature and limits of these Memoirs will not admit of a connected sketch of the American War, yet, as the motives that led to open hostilities, and the actions in which the first blood was shed, so peculiarly occupied the mind of a young Female, I cannot help following the example: especially as these were the opening of the great Drama, so singular in its nature and important in its consequences, and in which she afterwards became so distinguished an Actress.[17] These, added to a prompt regard and honor to the memory of those Heroes who fell the first sacri-

17 The long account which follows of the opening events of the American Revolution is omitted in the MS. memoir, as wholly irrelevant. It was evidently inserted here merely to fill up the space.

fices in the cause of their country, induce me to dwell for a few minutes on those scenes, the remembrance of which, while they fire the mind and passions with genuine love of liberty and patriotism, must bring up recollections shocking and melancholy to every tender mind.

The repeated and unjust Acts of Parliament, which they more strenuously endeavoured to enforce on the Colonies, seemed to threaten general destruction, unless they would, in One mutual Union, take every effectual method of resistance. For this purpose, a Congress had been formed, whose first business was to remonstrate and petition for redress. At the same time they had the precaution to take methods for defence, in case their voice should not be heard in Parliament. Great encouragement was given for the manufacture of all kinds of military stores and apparatus. The militia were trained to the use of arms.

Whilst things were going on in this manner, a detachment of troops commanded by Colonel Smith and Major Pitcairn were sent from Boston to possess or destroy some stores at Concord, twenty miles from Boston. At Lexington a few companies were collected for the purpose of manoeuvring, or to oppose the incursions of the British. These, as some accounts say, were ordered by the British commander, with the epithet of damn'd rebels, to disperse. Whether they so readily complied with the injunction as he wished, or not, he ordered his troops to fire upon them; and eight men were instantly the victims of death.

After the dispersion of the militia, the troops proceeded to Concord and destroyed a few stores. But by this time the militia had collected from the adjacent towns, and seemed unanimously resolved to avenge, by severe retaliation, the death of their innocent brethren. This the troops effectually experienced during their precipitate march to Boston.

Who but the actors and spectators, being themselves unaccustomed to scenes of this kind, can best describe the anguish of mind and emotions of passion excited by it! The loss of the Americans was small compared to the British. But view them once tranquil and happy in the midst of social and domestic compact. No music more harsh than the note of the shepherd, of friendship and innocent glee. With the lark each morn was welcomed, as a prelude to new joy and satisfaction.—Now behold the reverse of the scene! As if nature had been convulsed, and with just indignation had frowned on some unpardonable offence, their peace, and every social and private endearment was at once broken up. But she stands acquitted; whilst the pride of man could be satiated only with the dear price of the scourge—the havoc of war. On that fatal day when their fields and streets, which had so often re-echoed with rural felicity, suddenly assumed the aspect of the regular battalia, resounding with nothing but the din of war and the agonies of expiring relatives and friends, the Earth seemed to precipitate her diurnal revolution, and to leave the Sun in frightful aspect. The shepherd's flocks stood aghast. Birds forgot to carol, and hastened away with astonished muteness. And think—while the tender female breast turned from the scene in distraction, how it must have humanized the most savage temper, and have melted it into sympathy, even towards a relentless enemy.

The news of this battle spread with the rapidity of a meteor. All America was roused and many companies of militia from remote parts marched day and night, almost without intermission, to the relief of their friends in Massachusetts. Thus in a short time the environs of Boston exhibited, to the view of the enemy, the formidable appearance of 20,000 men.

This event had the same effect on the mind of Miss Sampson as it had on those of every one, that was awake to the introduction of objects so interesting and important, and whose feelings were ready to commiserate the sufferings of any of the human race.

On June the 5th, the same year, Congress unanimously appointed George Washington, Esq., to the chief command of the American Army. He is a native of Virginia and though he is a human being, his abilities and improvements can never be called in question. He had acquired great reputation in the execution of a Colonel's commission in the French war. He accepted this appointment with a diffidence which, while it best interpreted his wisdom, evinced the fidelity of his heart and his patriotic zeal for the fulfilment of the important trust reposed in him.*—Of this illustrious personage I may have further occasion to speak in the progress of these Memoirs.

Lexington battle was soon succeeded by that of Breed's Hill in Charlestown, Massachusetts, a mile and a half from Boston.

The 16th of this month, a detachment of Provincials under the command of Col. Prescott was ordered to intrench on Bunker's Hill the ensuing night. By some mistake, Breed's Hill was marked out for the intrenchment, instead of Bunker's, it being high and large like it, and on the furthermost part of the peninsula next to Boston. They were prevented going to work till midnight. They then pursued their business with alacrity and so profound was their silence, that they were not heard by the British on board their vessels lying in the harbour. At daybreak they had thrown up a small redoubt; which was no sooner noticed by the *Lively*, a man of war, than her cannon gave them a very heavy salute.

The firing immediately rouzed the British camp in Boston, and their fleet to behold a novelty they had little expected. This diverted their attention from a scheme they meant to have prosecuted the next day; which was now called to drive the Americans from the hill.

Notwithstanding an incessant cannonade from the enemy's ships, floating batteries and a fort upon Copp's hill in Boston, op-

*He arrived at Head Quarters in Cambridge on the 2d of July following.

posite the American redoubt, they continued laborious till noon, with the loss of only one man. By some surprising oversight. one detachment had labored incessantly four hours, with being relieved, or supplied with any refreshment.

By this time the Americans had thrown up a small breast-work, extending from the east side of their redoubt towards the bottom of the hill; but were prevented completing it by the intolerable fire of the enemy.

Just after twelve o'clock, the day fair and excessively hot, a great number of boats and barges were filled with regular troops and apparatus, who sail to Charlestown. The Generals Howe and Pigot take the command. After they were landed they form, and remain in that position till they are joined by another detachment, consisting of infantry, grenadiers and marines; which make in all about 3,000.

During these operations, the Generals Warren and Pomeroy join the American force. General Putnam continues ambitious in giving aid as occasion requires.[18] They are ordered to take up a post and rail-fence, and to set it not quite contiguous to another, and to fill the vacancy with some newly mown grass, as a slight defence to the musketry of the enemy. They are impatiently waiting the attack.

In Boston, the Generals Clinton and Burgoyne had taken their stand on Copp's Hill to contemplate the bloody operations now com-

18 General Joseph Warren was on the field that day, but with no asserted authority. On entering the redoubt thrown up by the troops, Colonel Prescott offered him the command; but Warren replied that he had not received his commission, and should serve as a volunteer. He had been chosen major-general by the Provincial Congress of Massachusetts only three days before. He gave no order during the action, though his presence and example were of great service. He took a musket, and mingled in the thickest of the fight.—[Frothingham's *Siege of Boston;* Loring's *Hundred Boston Orators.*]

General Seth Pomeroy, a veteran who had behaved with great gallantry at Louisburg, also served as a volunteer on Bunker Hill, and fought in the ranks with a musket in hand. He was at the rail-fence. General Israel Putnam was also at the rail-fence, in command of the Connecticut troops, and rendered important service.—[Frothingham's *Siege of Boston.*]

mencing. General Gage had previously determined, when any works should be raised in Charlestown by the Americans, to burn the town: and whilst his troops were advancing nearer to the American lines, orders came to Copp's Hill for the execution of the resolution. Accordingly a carcass was discharged, which sat fire to the hither part of the town; which being fired in other parts by men for that purpose, was in a few minutes in a general flame.

What scenes are now before us! There a handsome town, containing 300 houses, and about 200 other buildings, wrapt in one general conflagration; whose curling flames and sable smoke, towering to the clouds, seem to bespeak heavy vengeance and destruction! In Boston, see the houses, piazzas and other heights crowded with the anxious inhabitants, and those of the British soldiery, who are not called upon duty! Yonder the adjacent hills and fields are lined with Americans of both sexes, and of all ages and orders. Now turn to the American lines and intrenchments. Behold them facing the most formidable enemy, who are advancing towards them with solemn and majestic dignity! In a few moments, must be exhibited the most horrid and affecting scene that mankind are capable of producing!

Although the Americans are ill supplied with stores, and many of their muskets without bayonets, yet they are generally good marksmen, being accustomed to hunting. The British move on slowly, instead of a quick step. The provincials are ordered to reserve their fire till the troops advance within ten or twelve rods; when they begin a tremendous discharge of musketry, which is returned by the enemy, for a few minutes, without advancing a yard. But the stream of American fire is so incessant and does such astonishing execution, that the regulars break and fall back in confusion. They are again with difficulty rallied; but march with apparent reluctance to the intrenchments. The Americans at the redoubt, and those who are attacked by the British infantry in their lines leading from it to the water, are ordered, as usual, to reserve their fire.—The fence proves a poor shelter: and many are much more exposed than necessity obliges; so that the British cannot, in future, stigmatize them with the name of cowards, who will fly at the sight of a grenadier's cap, nor for fighting in an unfair manner. They wait till the enemy is within six rods; when the earth again trembles with their fire. The enemy are mown down in ranks and again are repulsed. General Clinton observes this, and passes over from Boston without waiting for orders. The British officers are heard to say, "It is downright butchery to lead the troops on afresh to the lines." But their honor is at stake, and the attack is again attempted. The officers are seen to use the most violent gestures with their swords to rally their troops: and though there is an almost insuperable aversion in them to renew the attack, the officers are once more successful. The Americans are in want of ammunition, but cannot procure any. Whilst they are ordered to retreat within the fort, the enemy make a decisive push: the officers goad on the soldiers with their swords—redouble their fire on all sides; and the redoubt is attacked on three sides at once. The Americans are unavoidably ordered to retreat, but they delay, and fight with the butt end of their guns, till the redoubt is two-thirds filled with regular troops. In their retreat, which led over a neck leading from Cambridge to Charlestown, they were again in the greatest jeopardy of being cut off by the *Glasgow* man of war, floating batteries, &c. But they effected it without much loss, and with greater regularity than could be expected from men who had never before seen an engagement. General Warren, being in the rear, was shot in the back part of his head; and having clapped his hand to the wound, dropped down dead.

The number of Americans engaged, including those who dared to cross the Neck and join them, was only 1,500. Their loss was small compared with the British. The killed, wounded and missing were 453; of which, 139 were slain. Of the British, the killed and wounded were 1,054; of which, 226 were killed.[19]

It has been said by a veteran officer, who was at the battles of Dettingen, Minden, and several others, in Germany, that for the time it lasted he never knew anything equal it. The British displayed great heroic bravery, and there was a perpetual sheet of fire from the Americans for half an hour; and the action was intensely hot for double that time.

Among the slain of the British, they particularly lament the deaths of Lieut. Col. Abercromby and Major Pitcairn, who occasioned the first shedding of blood at Lexington. Among the Americans, we lament, in particular, the fall of General Warren, the Colonels Gardner, Parker, Chelmsford, &c.[20] But the fall of General Warren is the most effectually felt. By his fall the public sustain the loss of the warm patriot and politician, the eminent orator and physician; with which were blended the other endearing and ornamental accomplishments. And though an amiable consort and a number of small children had rendered his existence more desirable, he distinguished himself this day, by fighting as a volunteer; and fell an illustrious example in the cause of liberty and the rights of man.

About this time the country inhabitants, near Boston, were frequently alarmed by idle and ignorant reports that the British

19 The British force in the battle was stated by General Gage, in his official account, as something over 2,000. It would seem, therefore, that half their number were killed or wounded. Stedman, Bissett, and LordMahon, British historians, say the British force was 2,000; Marshall, Ramsay, and Barry, Americans, and Thacher, in his "Military Journal," say 3,000. Contemporary MSS., and the Journal of the Provincial Congress, say, between 3,000 and 4,000. The American force was about 1,500.

20 General Warren was killed just as the Americans were leaving the well-contested field. It was with the greatest reluctance that he left the redoubt. He was retreating slowly, which brought him next to the British. Colonel Thomas Gardner of Cambridge, and Lieutenant-colonel Moses Parker, were mortally wounded. Gardner died, July 3; Parker died, a prisoner, July 4. Major Willard Moore, who that day led Doolittle's regiment, was also mortally wounded. There was no officer of the name of Chelmsford in the battle (See Frothingham's *Siege of Boston*).

troops had broken through the American lines, were penetrating, with the greatest rapidity into the country, ravaging, plundering and butchering all before them.  And more than once was Miss Sampson persuaded to join her female circle, who were as ignorant of what passed in the armies as herself, to seek security in the dreary desert or deserted cottage.  But she peculiarly noted the day of Breed's Hill engagement, as did many others, by the incessant roar of the cannon.  A fertile eminence, near which she lived, is a standing monument of the pensive thoughts and reflections she experienced during the melancholy day.[21]  She has said that for some days after the battle, having had an account of it, sleep was a stranger to her.  It seems, her attention was of a different nature from that of many of her sex and youth.  Whilst they were only dreading the consequences, she was exploring the cause of the eruption. This, as she had heard, or naturally apprehended would terminate, at least, in New England's wretchedness or glory.

It is indeed too much to sport with the lives of any animals. But when a large number of men, many of whom perhaps are involuntarily led into the field, and many more, without knowing or caring for what reason, march within a few paces of each other, that their lives may be made a fairer mark for the sport of the avarice, pride and ambition of a few licenced incendiaries—nature must recoil, or the whole system of intellects forget there is a higher dignity of man.

She had frequent opportunity of viewing the American soldiers, as they marched from one part to another.  One day, having gone some distance to see a number of regiments, her curiosity was arrested by an officer, who boasted much of his courage and heroic achievements.  A young female domestic being near him, he thus

21 The meaning is, she heard the cannon, on the day of the battle, from a hill near her residence.  The distance is at least thirty miles.  Besides the firing from the British ships and floating batteries, and from Copp's Hill, a furious cannonade was kept up on the American lines in Roxbury, to divert the attention of the right wing of the American army, and to prevent reinforcements being sent to the troops on Bunker Hill.

addressed her: "You Slut, why are you not better dressed when you come to see so many officers and soldiers!" Miss Sampson seeing her confused, thus replied to the arrogant coxcomb:— "Elegance in dress, indeed, Sir, becomes the fair, as well as your sex. But how must that soldier feel who values himself so highly for his courage, his great exploits, &c. (perhaps where there is no danger), should they forsake him in the field of battle!"

Hostilities having commenced throughout the Colonies, a new and effectual school was opened for the hero, politician and statesman; and which was a stimulation, even to the philosophic moralist. The consequence of which was the declaration of our Independence, July 4, 1776. This momentous event took place two hundred and eighty-four years after the discovery of America by Columbus —one hundred and seventy, since the first established settlement in Virginia—and a hundred and fifty-six since the settlement of Plymouth in Massachusetts; which were the first permanent settlements in North America. And whilst this Era will forever be held a Jubilee by every votary of American Freedom, it must bring to our minds two very affecting periods:—First, the time when we, with the most heart-felt satisfaction, acknowledged the sovereignty of our parent country: And secondly, when we were distressed, and like her dutiful offspring asked her lenity and compassion—but could not share, even in her parental affection!

But out of great tribulation, it is believed, anguish has not been the greatest result. Those necessitous events were doubtless conducive to the raising our Empire to that rare height of perfection in the moral, as well as in the political world, in which it now so conspicuously shines.

### CHAPTER IV

WE are now to view the state of Miss Sampson's mind comparable to him who has planned some great achievement, which he believes, will be of the greatest utility and importance to him; but who finds his opportunities, rather than abilities, inadequate to its completion. I know not that she ever was deserving the name of fickleness in her pursuits; yet, I have the strongest reason to conclude that her mind, during her juvenility, was so crowded with inventive ideas for improvements as to throw it into uncommon anxiety. And notwithstanding her invention proposed many schemes, yet, as they tended to the same comparative object, they ought rather to be applauded than aspersed. Neither would I think it gratifying to any to account for this upon any other score. To assign no other motive for these intellectual exertions than the attainment of gewgaws, superfluity in dress and the night consumption, would not only be doing injustice to her but mentioning a train of evils, which it must be confessed characterize too great a part of our youth at this day; and which every legislator should discourage, and every parent prohibit.

Before this time, Congress had taken effectual methods to encourage the manufacture of our own apparel, and every other consumption in America. And the reflection is pleasing, that Mr. Thomas's family was not the only one who had not the reformation to begin. As though they had always been apprehensive of the utility and honor they should gain by it, they had always practised it; and the voice of Congress was only a stimulation, so that Miss Sampson's employments were not much altered. And she has, somewhere, suggested—that had we continued this most laudable and ever-recommendable employment, in the same degree, to this day, we should not only have increased commerce with many foreign nations, but, have retained immense sums of money, which are now piled shining monuments of the opulence of other nations, and of our own vanity and inattention. In this opinion, I am confident, every well-wisher to his country is still ready to concur.*

Necessity, our dreadful, but useful friend, having taught us the advantages of our own manufactures for the support and conveniences of life, continued still favorable to our intellectual powers, and prompted them to the study of arts and sciences. The propriety of this is ratified by our Independence. Nor was Miss Sampson the only one who realized it, but she has often said, she hoped every one who had, or may have, the same propensities for it, may have freer access to it. Her situation of mind was very applicable to the maxim—"Learning has no enemy but ignorance." She was not now of age; but she resolved, when that period should arrive, to devise some more effectual method to attain it.

It is natural for fear to subside, when danger flees out at the door. This doubtless was the case with many good people in Massachusetts, after the seat of war was removed to distant parts; when they were not so suddenly alarmed by its havoc. To whatever degree this may have been the case with Miss Sampson, it appears that its first impressions, instead of being obliterated by time, were more strongly impressed on her mind. In fact, it seems she only needed a different formation to have demonstrated in actions what she was obliged to conceal through restraint of nature and custom.

Just before she was eighteen, 1779, she was employed, much

*Miss Sampson has just shown me pieces of lawn and muslin which were manufactured with her own hands, soon after the commencement of the war. I consider them as nothing more than specimens of Columbian abilities, genius and taste. It is wounding to me to hear—"We can buy cheaper than we can make." No doubt—And so long as we encourage foreign manufacture by sending them our specie, there is no doubt, but they can sell cheaper than we can make. And even when they have entirely drained us of our money, there will be one cheerful certainty left—they will laugh at our credulity.

to her liking, six months in the warm season, in teaching a public
school in Middleborough.[22] In this business, experience more
effectually convinced her, that her education, rather than her endowments, was inadequate to the task. But her success more than
equalled her expectations, both with regard to the proficiency of
her pupils, and the approbation of her employers.

The next season her engagement was renewed for the same
term in the same school. She now found her talk easier, and her
success greater, having had the advantage of a good man-school
the preceding winter. The employment was very agreeable to her;
especially as it was a source of much improvement to herself

Not far from this time, there began to be an uncommon agita-
tion among many people in her neighborhood; as had been, or soon
followed, in many towns in New England. This penetrating disorder was not confined to old age. It violently seized on the middle-
aged, and as she remarked, even children caught the contagion.
There are but few mischiefs that war is not capable of effecting.[23]

22 This school was taught in the warm season of 1779, when Deborah had completed her
eighteenth year. Until the age of eighteen, she was bound to the service of Mr. Thomas.
Her term of service was now expired, and she was at liberty. The school taught by her was at
the village of Middleborough Four Corners, two miles from the house of Deacon Thomas.
The house in which she taught stood on the spot where Major Tucker now resides; the building
having subsequently been removed to Water Street, and occupied as a dwelling-house. At
this time, she boarded in the house of Abner Bourne, which now stands opposite to Peirce
Academy.—[Rev. Stillman Pratt.]

The range of study in her school was not extensive; and it may be taken as a specimen of
the summer schools generally in New England at this time. The books used were "The New
England Primer," here and there a Spelling Book, "The Psalter," and a few Testaments. A
sheet of paper was sometimes allowed to the boys for the exercise of penmanship, while the
chief occupation of the girls was to learn to knit and sew! One forward lad brought to school
a dilapidated copy of Fisher's "Young Man's Best Companion." A few books which Deborah
brought to the school for her own improvement completed the catalogue. Such is the account
she gives in the MS. memoir, where it is implied, though not expressly stated, that "The Assembly's Catechism" was taught in this, as in other schools, every Saturday. When the editor
taught school, forty years ago, this was the practice in Massachusetts.

23 It is to be hoped that very few readers of this volume will sympathize with the ir-
religious spirit exhibited in these remarks, and in those which follow. They are very properly

But some well-minded people were ready to term this the working of the Spirit, of the Holy Ghost—a reformation in religion. Whether it originated from the unusual and influential exertions of the clergy, who took advantage of this unparalleled crisis to add to their number of converts in the Christian religion; or whether it was a voluntary act of the mind, or a natural cachexy, or whether it is a characteristic trait of the Divine Character—I have not time here to conjecture.

She was in the midst of it, and was excited to observe its opera tions. But she had the wise precaution to study well its purport,

omitted in the MS. memoir. The facts of the case, derived from authentic sources, were the following:—

During the ensuing autumn and winter, there was in Middleborough, and in several other towns, an unusual interest felt in the great concerns of religion. Notwithstanding the heavy pressure of the war, many of the people were led to feel that there are higher interests than those which pertain merely to the present life. Nothing, surely, could be more rational, nothing more capable of a satisfactory vindication. A revival of religion is the greatest blessing which can be bestowed upon any people. It is a mark of stupendous madness when immortal beings, ruined by sin, and hastening to the judgment, can remain, year after year, wholly indifferent and thoughtless. They are the fanatics who neglect the great salvation!

Many, both old and young, in Middleborough, at this time, were making the earnest inquiry, "What shall I do to be saved?" Among the number thus tenderly and solemnly affected was Deborah Sampson, the subject of our story, then nineteen years of age. At length she entertained the hope that she had experienced renewing grace and that her sins were forgiven. Ever since coming to live in Middleborough, at the age of eight years, she had attended public worship with the First Congregational Church in that town, whose meeting-house was at the "Upper Green," so called. This church, at the time indicated in the text, had no settled pastor.* The Rev. Abraham Camp, who was then preaching there, is said to have entertained a high opinion of Deborah's talents and character, and to have regretted her departure from the congregation; for, as the revival extended into other sections of the town, it was greatly promoted by the labors of Rev. Asa Hunt,† a Baptist minister in the south part of Middleborough, at a locality known as "The Rock," on the borders of Rochester. Deborah was induced to attend on his preaching, and not long after joined herself in covenant with his church. The Records of the First Baptist Church in Middleborough show that she was received by them as a member, November 12, 1780. She continued in that relation less than two years. It appears that she renounced her covenant with the Church, and learned to speak lightly of experimental religion.

*The First Church in Middleborough was organized December 26, 1694, although materials for a church had long existed. Rev. Sam'l Fuller, their first minister, (son of the excellent Dr. Samuel Fuller of the *Mayflower*), had preached in the town from 1679, and probably from the incorporation of the town in 1669. After the death of the Rev. Sylvanus Conant, in 1777, there was no settled minister there till 1781. Mr. Abraham Camp, a graduate of Yale College in 1773, was preaching to this church at the time mentioned in the text. The people were greatly interested in his preaching, and gave him a unanimous call to be their pastor, in February, 1779, and again called him, by a vote of twenty-two to five, in November, 1780. He concluded not to settle in Middleborough.

†Mr. Hunt was from Braintree, and was ordained at Middleborough, October 30, 1771; d. September 2, 1791.

rather than to suffer the fugitive to take her by surprise. But let its tendency have been what it might, it answered a good purpose for her. It served to rouze her attention, and to bring about these important enquiries:—From whence came man? What is his business? And for what is he designed? She considered herself as having been too inattentive to religion, which, as she had been taught and naturally conceived, is the most indispensable duty enjoined on man, both with regard to his well-being here, and to the eternal welfare of his immortal part.

But from her best conclusive arguments drawn from a contest of this nature, she saw no propriety in it. Reason being per verted or obstructed in its course, the whole system of intellects is thrown into a delirium. This being the case, as she conceived, in this outcry of religion, its subjects were of course, not only disqualified for useful business, which was certainly wanted at that time, if ever, but rendered totally incapacitated for the adoration and worship of Deity, in a manner becoming his dignity, or the dictates of sound reason.

At this age, she had not professionally united herself to any religious denomination;[24] as was the practice of many of her cotemporaries. She considered herself in a state of probation, and a free agent; and consequently at liberty to select her own religion. In this she was in a measure mistaken. Had her mind been free from the manacles of custom and unswayed by education, she might have boasted of an advantage superior to all others, and might per adventure, have entertained the world with a set of opinions different from all other sects and nations. But these were her combatants. As she advanced on the stage of life to establish a religion, her prospect was that of the Christian world and her assent to it was at once urged by her mode of education. Indeed this was the only religion of which she had any knowledge, except that which simple nature always teaches.

[24] So far is this from being true, that she professed to be a subject of the revival, and united herself to the Baptist Church, as already stated.

But her researches in Christianity did not occasion so much surprise to its votaries as they did to herself. On examination, instead of finding only one denomination, she must have been entertained—more probably, alarmed on finding almost an infinite num ber of sects which had sprung out of it, and in each sectary a different opinion—all right, infallibly right, in their own estimation. A great diversity of scenery in the same drama, or tragedy, upon the stage, perhaps has nothing in it wonderful or criminal. But a religion, which is believed to be of divine origin, even communicated directly from God to Man, consequently intended for the equal good of all, but still subject to controversy—differently construed and differently practised—she conceived, has every thing of the marvellous, if not of an inconsistent nature. Thus, when she would attach herself to one, the sentiments of a second would prevail, and those of a third would stagnate her choice: and for a while she was tempted to reject the whole till thorough examination and the aid of Him, who cannot err, should determine the best. And I am not certain there are not many, who have made their profession, who ought to disapprove her resolution.

To have called in question the validity and authenticity of the Scriptures would only have been challenging at least one half America, and a quarter of the rest of the globe to immediate combat; for which she had neither abilities nor inclination. She began to reflect, however, that the being bound to any set religion, by the force of man, would not only be an infraction of the laws of Nature, but a striking and effectual blow at the prime root of that liberty for which our nation was then contending.

I would not leave the public to surmise that she derived no advantage from Christianity. Though divines utterly disallow that the plan of the Gospel can be attained by the dim light of nature, or by the boasted schools of philosophy, yet, we have already found in these Memoirs, that, as feeble as they are, they lead without equivocation to the knowledge and belief of Deity, who every one acknowledges, is the first and great object of our reverence and devotion. Christian morality, she acknowledges with more warmth than I have known in many, who have had greater advantages of education. Setting aside the doctrines of total depravity, election, and a few others, which were always inadmissible by her reason, she is an adherent to its creed. By her dissidence she is willing, however, that her ignorance should be so far exposed to the public as to declare, that she knows not whether it is more from the light of Gospel revelation, or the force of education, that she is led to the assent of the fundamental doctrines of Christianity.[25]

This view of her religious sentiments will be concluded by the following summary of what she now believes to be genuine religion: and under whatever denomination it may fall, it must always continue without a precedent.

That religion which has a tendency to give us the greatest and most direct knowledge of Deity, of his attributes and works, and of our duty to Him, to ourselves and to all the human race, is the truest and best; and by which only we can have consciences void of offence.

I take the liberty to close this chapter with a few digressional remarks.

Sensible I am, that when we can be made sensible that religion in its truest sense, ought to be made the ultimate end and object of our pursuit—that it is the greatest requisite for our general felicity both here and in futurity;—or should it be found that, as we disregard, or attend to it, our temporal interest will be affected, as it is by our legislative government—I am inclined to believe, not a mystery, or hidden part in it will long remain unexplored, but established or rejected, as it may be deemed genuine. Civil government and religion have, briefly, this difference:—Civil govern-

25 The author here delivers his own sentiments rather than those of Deborah Sampson. He reminds us of the fable of the viper biting the file.

ment serves as a directory necessary for the accumulation and preservation of temporal interest and conveniencies for life: religion teaches us how to set a proper estimate on them and on all other enjoyments in life. It expands and elevates the mind to a sense and knowledge of Deity, and to the dignity of human nature. It pervades the whole soul, and fills it with light and love. It is a source from which only, can be derived permanent satisfaction, and teaches us the true end of our existence. For want of a knowledge or realization of this, into how many gross errors and absurdities have mankind inadvertently fallen, or inattentively been led. When impositions of this kind have been multiplied upon them, when they have been stigmatized by this name or by that, in matters of sentiment; seems they have rested comfortably easy, without enquiring into their truth or justice, or passed them off with flighty indifference. But touch our interest—that bright, momentary gem! the cheek is immediately flushed, and the whole heart and head are upon the rack—set to invention for redress. So contracted and interwoven with lucrative, fantastical gain are the views and pursuits of men.

CHAPTER V

Remarkable anxiety of Miss Sampson's mind relative to the War, and to gain a knowledge of her country. For once she is tempted to swerve from the sphere of her sex, upon the mere principle of gratifying curiosity and of becoming more effectually instrumental in the promotion of good. There are but two methods for the accomplishment of this, in which her inclinations lead her to concur. The first is that of travelling in the character of a gentleman. The second, that of taking an effective part in the Cause of her Country, by joining the Army in the character of a voluntary soldier. The latter, after many severe struggles between prudence, delicacy and virtue, she resolves to execute.

IT is impossible to conjecture what would have been Miss Sampson's turn of mind, had she obtained the most refined education. But it requires no great force of logic to discover her leading propensities in her present situation. She was formed for *enterprise:* and had fortune been propitious, she might have wanted limitations.

221

Among all her avocations and intervening occurrences in her juvenility, her thirst for knowledge and the prevailing American contest, appear, by her diurnals, to have held the most distinguished and important sway in her mind;—distinguished, because they were different from the generality of her sex;—important, because on that depended the future welfare and felicity of our country. Her resolutions on these accounts, and the execution of them will now employ our attention.

From the maturity of her years, observation and experience, she could determine with more precision on the nature of the war and on the consequence of its termination.   This may be said to be her logic:—If it should terminate in our subjection again to England, the abolition of our Independence must follow; by which we not only mean to be free, but to gain us the possession of Liberty in its truest sense and greatest magnitude; and thus secure to ourselves that illustrious name and rank, that adorn the nations of the earth.

This, and her propensities for an acquaintance with the geography of her country, were alternately severe in her mind.   Her taste for geography must have been chiefly spontaneous; as the study of it in books was unfashionable among the female yeomanry. I am happy to remark here, that this useful and delightsome science is now become a polite accomplishment for ladies.

It was now a crisis with her not often to be experienced: and though it was painful to bear, it was doubtless conducive to improvement.   Invention being upon the rack, every wheel in the machine is put in motion, and some event must follow.   It produced many pertinent thoughts on the education of her sex.   Very justly did she consider the female sphere of action, in many respects too contracted; in others, wanting limits.   In general she deemed their opportunities, rather than abilities, inadequate for those departments in science and the belles-lettres, in which they are so peculiarly calculated to shine,   From this, let me infer that, although custom constitutes the general standard of female education, yet the best method that occurs to my mind to be used in this important business, is that dictated by reason and convenience.

But the public must here be surprised in the contemplation of the machinations and achievements of female heroism and virtue: which if not the most unparalleled, are the most singular that have ever sprung out of Columbia's soil. And it is but reasonable, that we exercise all that candor and charity, that the nature of the circumstances will admit. By ideally putting ourselves in similar circumstances the reasonableness will be fully evinced. Though independent and free, custom in many respects rules us with despotie sway; and the person who greatly deviates from it exposes himself to numberless dangers. An indelible stigma may doom him to infamy; though perhaps his original design was to effect some useful and important event. But on the other hand, liberty gives us such ascendancy over old habit, that unless it bind us to some apparent and permanent good, its iron bands are subject to dissolution. We have, in some measure seen Miss Sampson's motives for achievement; the rest will be illustrated in the sequel.

Having come of age, her former resolution* remained to be executed.[26] For this purpose she planned many schemes and fabricated many castles; but on examination found them chimerical, or of precarious foundation. Every recent information of the geography of the continent served only to stimulate propensities which she had no desire to stifle. But the news of the war served but to engross her mind with anxieties and emotions she had long labored to suppress. And it must here be mentioned to her honor, that she used arguments for and against herself in every important proposition drawn for enterprise. Her chief problems for solution may have been these: Must I forever counteract inclination

*See Chap. IV.

26 Her resolution to travel, and to obtain a knowledge of her country, induced her to enlist in the Continental army.

and stay within the compass of the smoke of my own chimney?
never tread on different soils nor form an acquaintance with a
greater circle of the human race?  Stifle that spirit of heroic patriotism, which no one knows but Him who foreknows all events but
may terminate in the greatest good to myself, and in some degree
promote the cause of my country?  Yield the palm of custom to
the force of that philanthropy which should warm the bosoms of
both sexes and all ages?—In fact, shall I swerve from my sex's
sphere for the sake of acquiring a little useful acquisition; or shall
I submit (without reluctance, I cannot) to a prison, where I must
drag out the remainder of my existence in ignorance: where the
thoughts of my too cloistered situation must forever harass my
bosom with listless pursuits, tasteless enjoyments and responsive
discontent?

Contrasting this argumentation with the superior advantages
of many of the human race for acquiring knowledge, she was
ready, for a moment, to find fault with her formation: but happily
it was but momentary.  As if she had been instantly cured of a
frenzy, she could scarcely be reconciled with herself for such presumption.  It being not only an indignity to her own sex, but the
basest ingratitude to her Maker, and derogatory to his laws.  Her
humble solicitations were, that she never might be so lost to all
sense of virtue and decorum, as to act a part unworthy her being,
thereby not only bring infamy on herself, but leave a blemish and
stigma on the female world.

For this purpose, she resolved to think no more of projecting
adventures, of leaving the tranquillity of her domestic retirement
—her endearing circle of relations and friends, to visit distant
parts; as the good she anticipated in the result was uncertain, and
might, in a fatal manner, prove fallacious.  Her flights of imagination had furnished a clue the most requisite for the maxim, which
every one more or less needs—"When fancy rides, let reason hold
the reins."  She likewise resolved to suspend all further enquiries

and anxiety about the war. Vain attempts! The prohibitions proved a source of mortification and discontent. And it seems, a prevention of these enquiries would have been as much impossible as it would to have brought the war to a close without negotiation, or by inaction itself. It seems, she could not hear of its success without feeling the victory. She had heard of many beautiful cities, rich soils, healthy climates and different customs with the inhabitants, and the thought of being prohibited from augmenting her acquaintance with them, was but anticipating her dissolution too soon.[27]

In this dilemma she continued several months without any fixed resolution. At length, her propensities for viewing distant places, &c. gained such a perfect ascendancy over cooler reason, that her propensities could brook no control. She determined to burst the bands which, it must be confessed, have too often held

[27] While Deborah, as in the text, is pondering her future course, let us consider what she was at this time.

She was now a few months over twenty years of age; had been deprived of the advantages resulting from a proper training under the parental roof, and, in great measure, of opportunities for intellectual improvement. She had good natural capacity; was of a studious, contemplative turn of mind; an ardent lover of nature; a careful observer of passing events. She was fond of adventure, and had a great deal of energy. Her temper was bold, enterprising, independent, fearless; and she was disposed to have her own way, regardless of consequences. The sphere in which she had hitherto moved she found too quiet and too narrow for her aspiring temperament: she longed for something higher and better, she knew not what. Under proper culture and discipline, she might have become an ornament to her sex and a blessing to the world. But she had none to guide, to train, to admonish her, scarcely any to sympathize with her. Consequently, her efforts were misdirected, her energies misemployed. To a considerable extent, she was a day-dreamer, and a builder of castles in the air. She had a strong desire to see the world, to visit distant regions, to behold society in new lights and under unusual aspects. She determined that she would, at all events, quit the ignoble employments to which she had been accustomed in a farmer's family in Middleborough,—of feeding pigs and poultry, of plying the spinning-wheel and the loom.

She resolved, therefore, to put on male attire, and travel; and to this end spun and wove, with her own hands, cloth, which (she says) she employed a tailor to make up as a suit for a gentleman, pretending that it was for a young man, a relative of hers, who was about leaving home for the army. She found these garments became her so well, that even her mother, whom she visited at Plympton in this costume, did not know her.ᐟ This is the statement which is made in the MS. memoir, where it is also stated that she procured and put on these garments several times, to try them, in the autumn of 1780. It was certainly a year later when this was done.

her sex in awe, and in some mode and measure, stretch beyond the boundaries of her own neighborhood; by which means she might be convinced whether what she had read or heard be true—"That one half of the world does not know how the other half lives." But here fresh scenes of difficulties awaited her; though many had been before anticipated. Prudence, as usual, appeared in her plain, but neat attire, and called her resolution in question. Delicacy trimmed her dislocated hair; and virtue brought her amaranthine wreath. The thought of travelling without a companion or protector, was deemed by prudence a step of presumption. Not to have travelled at all, might have deprived her of much good, with increasing anxiety; and there was an avenue to it both ways. But her greatest obstacle was the want of that current specie, which is always sure to gain the esteem of all people. Without it, she must have been liable to have incurred the appellation of an idler, a *bonaroba*, or a vagabond, and so have failed in her design, which was the acquisition of knowledge without the loss of reputation.

Whilst she was deliberating on these matters, she privately dressed herself in a handsome suit of man's apparel and repaired to a prognosticator.[28]  This, she declares, was not to stimulate, but to divert her inclinations from objects which not only seemed presumptuous, but impracticable.  She informed him she had not come with an intention to put entire confidence in his delusory suggestions; but it was partly out of principle, but mostly out of curiosity. He considered her as a blithe and honest young gentleman.  She heard his preamble.  And it was either by art or accident, that he told her, pretty justly, her feelings—that she had propensities for uncommon enterprises, and pressed to know why she had held them in suspension so long.  Having predicated, that the success of her adventures, if undertaken, would more than compensate a few difficulties, she left him with a mind more discomposed than when she found him.  But before she reached home she found her

---

28  Or fortune-teller.  Her interview with him undoubtedly contributed much to strengthen and confirm her resolution.

resolution strengthened. She resolved soon to commence her ramble, and in the same clandestine plight, in which she had been to the necromancer. She thought of bending her first course to Philadelphia, the metropolis of America.

In March, 1781, the season being too rough to commence her excursion, she proposed to equip herself at leisure, and then appoint the time for her departure. A handsome piece of cloth was to be put to a use of which she little thought, during the time she was employed in manufacturing it. Ye sprightly Fair, what is there in your domestic department that necessity, ingenuity and resolution cannot accomplish?—She made her a genteel coat, waistcoat and breeches without any other assistance, than the uncouth patterns belonging to her former master's family. The other articles, hat, shoes, &c. were purchased under invented pretexts.[29]

Before she had accomplished her apparatus, her mind being intent, as the reader must imagine, on the use to which they were soon to be appropriated, an idea no less singular and surprising than true and important, determined her to relinquish her plan of travelling for that of joining the American Army in the character of a voluntary soldier.[30] This proposal concurred with her

[29] During her abode in the family of Mr. Thomas, he had allowed her the income arising from a number of fowls and sheep, with the understanding that it should be applied to useful purposes. The burning of Charlestown and the siege of Boston had occasioned severe suffering to the inhabitants of those places; and Deborah had contributed out of her scanty stock for their relief. This small fund also enabled her to purchase the materials for a suit of masculine apparel. During several weeks of the winter, she was employed in spinning and weaving a piece of handsome woolen cloth. As spring advanced, and the weather became more comfortable, she retired, as we are informed, to a beautiful recess in the grove above the Borden Hills, and there, with the aid of patterns, cut and made for herself a coat, vest, and breeches. (Pantaloons reaching to the ankles were not then worn.)—[Rev. S. Pratt.]

[30] Her original plan of travelling as a gentleman was soon laid aside, from the lack of that very necessary article, which, as the royal preacher well says, "answereth all things." There remained no other method for gratifying the roving propensities which had now acquired full possession of her mind, but this,—to enlist as a soldier in the Continental army. There is no need of denying that she felt also the impulse of earnest and genuine patriotism; but this seems not to have been the principal motive. From the beginning of the Revolutionary struggle, she had, though a young girl, sympathized intensely with the cause of liberty, and had, with

inclinations on many accounts. Whilst she should have equal
opportunities for surveying and contemplating the world, she
should be accumulating some lucrative profit; and in the end, perhaps, be instrumental in the cause of liberty, which had for nearly
six years enveloped the minds of her countrymen.

Here I might bring forward her former monitors, and repre
sent the affecting dialogues which no virtuous mind wishes to dis
pute, she held with them on this trying occasion. But I leave this
for the poet, novelist, or some more able pen. Suffice it to say, the
following motto is the chief result of her debates:—"There may be
an heroic innocence as well as an heroic courage." Custom, not
virtue, must lose its name by transition; unless custom be made
the criterion of virtue. She debated, with all the force of eloquence that a sense of duty to a parent or mistress could produce,
whether to communicate her intentions to them, or to make a confident of any one in so important an undertaking. She resolved in
the negative, for this reason:—If her pursuits should terminate in
an event that should cause her to lament her engagement, she
should not reflect upon herself for having gone counter to their
advice and injunctions; though she might, for not asking and ad-
hering to them. In either case, she meant to make an expiation.

Females! _you_ have resolutions and you execute them. And
you have, in a degree, the trial of the virtues and graces, that adorn
your sex. Then, by ideal similitude, put yourselves in the situation of our Heroine (for thus she must be distinguished in future),
and then grant her such favors as you might wish from her. I
am your friend, and would do honor to that which dignifies your
character, and renders you the amiable companions of man. Heaven
who has aided Columbia's Cause, recognize my sincerity! And although it has been purchased, mostly, at the dear expense of her

deep emotion, listened, from a hill near her residence, to the boom of cannon on the day of Bunker Hill.

It seems very clear that an enlistment as a soldier was not the original plan, nor patriotism
the original impulse.

sons; you have not remained uninterested nor without the pang of the distressed lover.—I cannot desire you to adopt the example of our Heroine, should the like occasion again offer; yet we must do her justice. Whether that liberty which has now cemented us in so happy an union, was purchased through direct, or indirect means, we certainly owe the event to Heaven. And enterprise in it can better be dispensed, than in many other eminent cases. Let your imagination, therefore, travel with me through the toils and dangers she has passed. And if you exercise that propriety and sweetness of temper which I have known in many of you, in the contemplation of other less interesting scenes and objects, I am sure, I shall never be tired with your company.

## CHAPTER VI

The time prefixed for her personating the soldier. Reflections on her bidding adieu to her relations, friends, &c. Takes a Western, circuitous route for Boston. Is hired for a class of Uxbridge, as a soldier, for three years, or during the War. Her mode of joining the Army at West Point. Is put into the Fourth Massachusetts Regiment.

IN April, 1781, having obtained what requisites she could for her new but hazardous expedition, warm weather being generally settled—she allowed herself but a few days to compromise matters with herself, and to take a private leave of her agreeable circle, before her departure.[31] The thoughts of being put into a kind of transformation were not so alarming as the dread fatality, which she knew not but it might produce. Whilst most females must recoil at the commencement of an undertaking of this nature, few can have resolution to attempt a second trial. And had I a tragic-comic pen, it might find ample scope in the scenes now before me.

31 It has been satisfactorily and conclusively shown in the Introduction, by official documents, that "her departure" was in May, 1782.

Several circumstances concurred, in this interim, which could not have failed to excite peculiar emotions. She knew her mother had long doted on her future felicity with a young gentleman of fortune, and agreeable deportment; and with whom she had contracted an intimate and endearing acquaintance. He had given her many cordial proofs of the sincerity of his attachment and lasting affections. And had her mind been disencumbered with a higher object in view, she might, doubtless, have united her affections in the happiest alliance for life.[32] Already did she consider a parent not only disappointed in her warmest wishes, but distracted with anguish by the elopement, and for aught she knew, the fatal and untimely catastrophe of a daughter. She felt for those who had taken the charge of her youth;[33] whose affections had not been alienated by her disobedience. For him who loved her, she felt with emotions that had not before alarmed her. Indeed, such groups of ideas that hurried upon her mind must have been too much for a breast naturally tender. She retired to indulge the effects of nature, and in this seclusion, resolved, should her pursuit succeed, to write to her mother in a manner that might pacify her mind without disclosing the delicate stratagem.

32 That this talk about the "young gentleman of fortune" is mere "moonshine," will be apparent from a quotation from the MS. memoir, to which I have repeatedly referred. She says,

"I did not, however, in this vernal season of raptures and despairs, escape the addresses of a young man, of whom my mother, I believe, was passionately fond, and seemed struck with wonder that I was not. She considered him regenerated. I had not her eyes to see such perfection in this lump of a man, or that he possessed qualities that would regenerate me. I had no aversion to him at first, and certainly no love, if I have ever understood that noble passion. At any rate, this marry, or not to marry, was decided thus: On a certain parade day he came to me, with all the *sang froid* of a Frenchman, and the silliness of a baboon, intoxicated, not with love, but with rum. From that moment I set him down a fool, or in a fair way to be one."

This will serve to show that "The Female Review" cannot, in matters of detail, be safely trusted.

It is quite probable that a wish to escape the addresses of this young man—though he is doubtless grossly misrepresented in the extract just made—was one of the motives which operated in inducing her to leave home secretly, and join the army.

33 The family of Deacon Thomas, next to her mother, her best friends.

But neither the rigor of a parent to induce her marriage with one whom she did not dislike, nor her own abhorrence of the idea of being considered a female candidate for conjugal union, is the cause of her turning volunteer in the American War; as may hereafter partly be conjectured by an anonymous writer. This must be the greatest obstacle to the magic charm of the novelist. She did not slight love, nor was she a distracted inamorata. She considered it a divine gift: nor was she deceived. For, strike love out of the soul, life becomes insipid and the whole body falls into lethargy. Love being always attended by hope, wafts us agreeably through life. She was a lover; but different from those whose love is only a short epilepsy, or for the gratification of fantastical and criminal pleasure. This I trust will be demonstrated by a fact, to which, but few can appeal. Her love extended to all. And I know not but she continues to have this consoling reflection, that no one can tax her for having coveted the prohibited enjoyment of any individual. This is that love, whose original source and mo tive induced Columbia's sons to venture their property, endear ments—their lives! to gain themselves the possession of that heaven-born companion called liberty: and which, when applied to conjugal union, is the same thing, only differently combined with the other passions. And whatever effect it may then have had on her, she has since been heard to say, without reserve that she deemed it more honorable for one to be suffocated with the smoke of cannon in the Cause in which she was then embarked, than to waste a useful intended existence in despair, because Heaven had justly denied the favorite of a whimsical and capricious fancy. The perseverance for the object, dictated by love in both cases, corroborates beyond doubt its efficacy and utility.

Just before her departure, she received a polite invitation to join a circle of her acquaintance for rural festivity. She was cheerful; and the rest of the company more so. Among many lively topics, it was remarked that Mr.————, brother to a lady not present, had been killed in the battle at Long Island, in New York. It was brushed into oblivion by concluding—his sweetheart was again courted. It drew involuntary tears from our intended heroine, which were noticed. In the evening, she returned home with emotions that might affect a lover.

Next day the weather was exceedingly pleasant; and nature smiled with the season. Miss Sampson performed her business with much affected gaiety and sprightly conversation but the night was to be big with the important event.[34]

34 I am sorry to spoil a good story; but there is another account given of her assumption of male attire, far less romantic than that given in the text, and far more trustworthy. It was given to my friend, Rev. Stillman Pratt, by a person in Middleborough who remembered Deborah Sampson. It is also for substance confirmed by that distingusihed antiquary, Mr. Samuel G. Drake of Boston, whose first wife was a near relative of Capt. Leonard. The account is as follows:—

During the war of the Revolution, Capt. Benjamin Leonard, a distant connection of Hon, Daniel Leonard of Taunton, the author of the famous letters signed "Massachusettensis,' resided in Middleborough, eastwardly from what are now known as the Upper Namasket Works. A negro woman of the name of Jennie, daughter of a slave of Judge Oliver, was an inmate of his family. Here Deborah Sampson was staying for a time. By the aid of this negro woman, Deborah dressed herself in a suit of clothes belonging to a young man named Samuel Leonard, a son of Capt. Benjamin Leonard. Thus clad, she repaired to a recruiting-office, kept at the house of Mr. Israel Wood. There she enlisted as a soldier under the assumed name of Timothy Thayer, and received the bounty. Having now plenty of money, she went, thus attired, to a tavern near the meeting-house, two miles east of Middleborough Four Corners; called for spirituous liquors; got excited; and behaved herself in a noisy and indecent manner. During the night she returned home; crept to bed with the negro; and when morning came resumed her female attire, and returned to her female employments, as if nothing had happened.

She enlisted at this time, it is supposed, partly to have a little frolic, and to see how it would seem to put on a man's clothing, but chiefly for the purpose of procuring a more ample supply of spending money. Some of the money she now received was spent for female wearing apparel. A few nights after this adventure, she appeared at a singing-school, held at a house near the present residence of Mr. Earle Sproat, dressed out in a somewhat gaudy style. On this occasion, she made a present of a pair of long gloves to a young lady of her acquaintance, to whom she felt indebted for special kindness in a time of sickness.

She had doubtless long meditated the design of becoming a soldier, but was not yet quite prepared to join the army. It was now either in the winter season, or the early spring of 1782; and it seemed best to wait a while.

When the time came for the soldiers newly enlisted in Middleborough to join their regiment, Timothy Thayer, to the surprise of the recruiting-officer, could not be found. His iden-

Having put in readiness the materials she had judged requisite, she retired at her usual hour, to bed, intending to rise at twelve. She was doubtless punctual.   But there was none, but the Invisible, who could take cognizance of the effusions of passion on assuming her new garb; but especially on reflecting upon the use for which it was assigned—on leaving her connections, and even the vicinity, where the flower of her life had expanded and was then in its bloom.   She took her course towards Taunton in hopes of meeting with some stranger, who was going directly to Head Quarters, then at the Southward.[35]—Having walked all night she was just entering the Green in Taunton, when the bright luminary of day,

tity with Deborah Sampson was discovered in this manner: When the supposed Timothy was putting his name to the articles of enlistment, an old lady, who sat near the fire carding wool, remarked that he held the pen just as Deb. Sampson did.   Deborah, having by means of a felon, or whitlow, lost the proper use of her fore-finger, was obliged to hold a pen awkwardly when she wrote.   This was well known in the neighborhood where she had kept school, and where, of course, she had often been seen to use a pen.   This circumstance led to a strong suspicion that she and Timothy Thayer were the same person.   Inquiry being made, black Jennie disclosed the part she had acted in dressing Deborah in men's clothes.   Deborah, thus exposed, was obliged to refund that portion of the bounty-money she had not spent, and to keep herself out of sight for a time, lest punishment should overtake her.   Traditiou affirms that Samuel Leonard was so shocked at the idea of his clothes having been used by a woman, that he never wore them afterwards.

There is no reason, however, to doubt that she provided herself with a suit of masculine apparel, by the labor of her own hands, in the manner already stated.   If her scheme was to be put in execution, she must of course have a suit of her own.   The clothes of Samuel Leonard were put on merely for the occasion, and she had no intention of keeping them.   The frolic in which they were used occurred some months before her second enlistment.

The assurance given by the fortune-teller whom she visited, as stated on page 84, that she would succeed in the plan she was meditating, seems to have contributed to confirm her resolution to join the American army.   Her repeated experiments in male attire had been successful: she had passed for a man without suspicion; and, as she says in the MS. memoir, she found men's clothes more convenient than those worn by her own sex.   It was not without considerable hesitation and misgiving that the final resolution was taken.   The family of Deacon Thomas had been kind to her; she had not alienated their affections even by her wayward conduct; and to leave them utterly cost her a severe struggle.   What troubled her most of all was the thought that her mother, who still lived in Plympton, would be distressed at her disappearance.   At last however she came to the fixed determination to join the army, and abide the consequences.

35 Taunton Green, which is the principal village in Taunton, is eight or ten miles from Middleborough, on the west.

which had so often gleamed upon her in the rusticity of a shepherdess, then found her, not indeed impressed only with the simple care of a brood of chickens or a bleating lamb—but with a no
less important Cause than that in which the future felicity of America was then suspended.  The reflection startled her: but female
temerities were not to be palliated.

At this instant, she unwelcomely met Mr. William Bennett,
her near neighbor.  Surely, an apoplexy could not have given her
a more sudden shock.[36]  Though she was not positive he had discovered her masquerade, yet she knew if he had, she should be pursued when he reached home.  After some refreshment, and supply-
ing her pockets with a few biscuit, she hastened through the town,
but determined not to bend her course directly for the Army, till
she should know what had been done about her clandestine elopement.  Fatigued with walking she took an obscure path, that led
half a mile into a thicket of wood, where the boughs of a large
pine served for her canopy during her repose till evening.  Surprised
when she awoke on finding it dark, with difficulty she regained the
road; and by the next peep of dawn found herself in the environs
of her former neighborhood.[37]

Dejected at the sight of the place where she had enjoyed so
much rural felicity, she half resolved to relinquish all thoughts of
further enterprize, and to palliate what had passed as a foible,
from which females are not always exempt.  The debate was not
long.  As usual, she must persevere and make the best of what
might prove a bad choice.  The groves were her sanctuary for
meditation that day and the succeeding night.  After the birds
had sung their evening carols, she lay down with intentions to

36 Her eye met his; her heart palpitated: she feared that she was known; but she passed
by him without discovery.

37 Her heart now began to fail her.  Fearing that Mr. Bennett had penetrated her disguise, and that her friends would start in hot pursuit, she retraced her steps to Middleborough
to learn if any thing of the kind were in progress.  Finding no evidence of pursuit, she resolved
to persevere in her romantic undertaking, but started in another direction.

sleep: but necessity, our old alarming friend, roused her attention. Impelled by hunger, during the tranquillity of the village she repaired to a house she had much frequented, with intentions to appease the cravings of nature. Going to a pantry where victuals was wont to be deposited, and meeting with no better success than a crust of bread, she again retired to her solitary asylum—the caroling of the feathered tribe having again noticed her of day, she resumed her ramble and soon lost sight of those

> Adjacent villas, long to her endear'd,
> By the rough piles our ancestors have rear'd.

She reached Rochester that day, and the next, Bedford, a seaport town in Massachusetts; which had been much distressed by the British in 1778-79. She here met with an American, Commander of a cruiser; who, after much importunity and proffered emolument, gained her consent to go [as] his waiter to sea. But she was informed that, although he used much plausibility on the shore, it was changed to austerity at sea.[38] She therefore requested him to keep her month's advance, and leave to go into town on business, and that night lodged in Rochester, and was careful not to see him afterwards.*

Hearing nothing concerning her elopement, she concluded to take a circuitous ramble through some of the Western towns and visit Boston, the capital of Massachusetts, before she joined the army. This was partly to gratify curiosity and partly to familiarize herself to the different manners of mankind—a necessary qualifica-

*It has been reported, that she enlisted, as a Continental Soldier, for a class in Middleborough—that she received a part of the stipulated bounty—that she was immediately discovered, and refunded the bounty. I have no account of this from her; nor is the report in the least authenticated. It probably has since taken its rise from this circumstance.[39]

38 Rochester joins Middleborough on the south. At a tavern in that place, where she spent the next night, she saw some of her town's-people, without being known by them. The next day she reached New Bedford, where she enlisted on board of a privateer, but abandoned the design on being informed of the captain's bad treatment of his men.

39 For proof of the correctness of this "report," see note 34.

tion for a soldier, and perhaps not detrimental to any whose minds are properly fortified, and whose established maxim is—To do good.

She left Rochester on Friday. The next night and the succeeding, she tarried at Mr. Mann's tavern in Wrentham. From thence she visited some of the Western towns in the State.[40] Finding herself among strangers, her fear of being discovered subsided, and she found herself in an element from which she had long involuntarily been sequestered. She doubtless, had awkward gestures on her first assuming the garb of the man; and without doubt more awkward feelings. Those who are unacquainted with masquerade must make a difference between that which is only to heighten beauty for fantastical amusement and pleasure— and that of sex, which is to continue perhaps for life, to accomplish some important event. She acted her part: and having a natural taste for refinement she was everywhere received as a blithe, handsome and agreeable young gentleman.

It may be conjectured whether or not she meant to see the army before she enlisted. By what follows it appears she did not. She doubtless chose to engage for Massachusetts; not because she could render any more service, but because it is her native State, and which had been the opening of the first scene of the horrid drama, and had suffered most by its actors.

In Bellingham she met with a speculator, with whom, for a certain stipulated bounty,* she engaged for a class of Uxbridge as

---

*General Washington refused any pecuniary pay for his services during the war. Our Heroine needed, at least, his wealth, to have followed the example.

40 This is not true. From Wrentham, where she spent two days, she went to Boston, travelling, as before, all the way on foot. She then passed through Roxbury, Dedham, and Medfield, to Bellingham; wishing to proceed a considerable distance from home before she enlisted. In Bellingham she met with a recruiting-officer; and, being at this time almost destitute of money, she enlisted as a soldier, under the assumed name of Robert Shurtliffe. This was the name of her elder brother.—[MS. Memoir.]

a Continental Soldier.†[41] Instead then of going to Boston, she went back and was immediately conducted to Worcester, where she was mustered. She was enrolled by the name of Robert Shurtliffe. The general muster-master was doubtless glad to enrol the name of a youth whose looks and mien promised to do honor to the cause, in which she was then engaged.[42] Ah, females—we have too long estimated your abilities and worth at too mean a price! Pardon an inadvertent misapplication of our intellects; as our profession is improvement, and our propensities to redress all wrongs.

On May 13th, she arrived at West Point in company with about fifty other soldiers, who were conducted there by a sergeant sent for that purpose.[43] West Point was then an important post, where was stationed a large division of the American army. It guarded a passage in the river Hudson, sixty miles from the city of New York. West Point will forever remain distinguished by the infamous treason of General Arnold in 1780. His conduct, the

†Those are called Continental Soldiers, who engaged for three years, or during the war.

41 The male population of every town, capable of bearing arms, was at that time divided into classes, as they were called; and each class was obliged to furnish a soldier for the army. The class sometimes paid a very considerable bounty. Deborah enlisted, and was accepted, for a class in Uxbridge. The enlistment was for three years, or during the war. Bellingham is separated from Uxbridge by the town of Mendon. The man who enlisted Deborah is called a speculator, because he withheld from her a part of the bounty-money to which she was entitled.

42 The muster-master was Capt. Eliphalet Thorp of Dedham, whose certificate has already been given in the Introduction. From his certificate it appears that she enlisted May 20, 1782; more than a year later than is stated in the context, page 16.

The story told by Mrs. Ellet about Deborah's passing seven weeks after her enlistment in the family of Capt. Nathan Thayer in Medway, and the "love passage" between the supposed Robert Shurtliffe and a girl visiting the family, appears to be destitute of any foundation.

43 In the MS. memoir, she says that this march of ten or twelve days was very fatiguing to her. At the close of a chill and drizzly day, on approaching a fire in a tavern, she fainted, and fell upon the floor. Recovering, she found herself surrounded by kind spirits ministering to her relief. Particularly she noticed a beautiful young woman, the innkeeper's wife, who offered her cordials and refreshments, with many expressions of pity and sympathy that one so young and tender should suffer the hardships of such a march. This amiable lady insisted that the delicate young recruit should take her place in the bed with her husband. In the memoir, the account of the march is highly colored.

preceding winter in the city of Philadelphia, had been censured; which gave him offence. The consequence was he sought for re venge. He conspired with Sir Henry Clinton to deliver West Point and all the American army into the hands of the British; which he meant to accomplish during General Washington's absence in Connecticut. But the plot was providentially disconcerted. Major André, Adjutant General in the British army, an illustrious young officer, had been sent as a spy to concert the plan of operations with Arnold. On his return he was overtaken, condemned by a court-martial, and executed.* Arnold made his escape by getting on board the *Vulture*, a British vessel but his character wears a stigma, which time can never efface.

In the morning, she crossed the Hudson near Fort Clinton. This is one of the most beautiful and useful rivers in the United States. It takes its name, as do many others in America, from its discoverer. Its source is between the lakes Ontario and Champlain, running in a southern direction two hundred and fifty miles, till it falls into the ocean, where it forms a part of New York harbor. It is navigable for ships of almost any burthen to the city of the same name, a hundred and thirty-six miles from its mouth.

They marched on level land, and quickly had orders to parade for inspection. The soldiers were detached into their proper companies and regiments. It fell to her lot to be in Capt. Webb's company of light infantry, in Col. Shepard's regiment, and in General Paterson's Brigade.[44]

*A particular account of his behaviour, from the time he was captured to his execution, would heave the most stubborn bosom and affect the magnanimous mind.

44 Our heroine enlisted in the Fourth Massachusetts Regiment, commanded at that time by Col. William Shepard of Westfield, but soon afterwards by Col. Henry Jackson of Boston. This regiment was the old Ninth. Col. Shepard had command of it from 1777 to 1782. George Webb was one of the captains.

Col. William Shepard was born December 1, 1737, son of Deacon John Shepard. He entered the army at the age of seventeen; was in 1759, a captain under Gen. Amherst in the old French war; and was in various battles, as at Fort William Henry, Crown Point, &c. He

The second day she drew a French fusee, a knapsack, cartridge-box, and thirty cartridges. Her next business was to clean her piece, and to exercise once every morning in the drill, and at four o'clock, P. M. on the grand parade. Her garb was exchanged for a uniform peculiar to the infantry. It consisted of a blue coat lined with white, with white wings on the shoulders and cords on the arms and pockets; a white waistcoat, breeches or overhauls and stockings, with black straps about the knees; half boots, a black velvet stock, and a cap, with a variegated cockade on one side, a plume tipped with red on the other, and a white sash about the crown. Her martial apparatus, exclusive of those in marches, were a gun and bayonet, a cartridge box and hanger with white belts. She says she learned the manual exercise with facility and dispatch, though she lost her appetite; which, through favor, she afterwards recovered.

Her stature is perhaps more than the middle size; that is, five feet and seven inches. The features of her face are regular; but not what a physiognomist would term the most beautiful. Her eye is lively and penetrating. She has a skin naturally clear, and flushed with a blooming carnation. But her aspect is rather masculine and serene, than effeminate and sillily jocose. Her waist might displease a coquette: but her limbs are regularly proportioned. Ladies of taste considered them handsome, when in the masculine garb.* Her movement is erect, quick and strong: gestures naturally mild, animating and graceful; speech deliberate, with firm articulation. Her voice is not disagreeable for a female.

married Sarah Dewey, who was his wife fifty-seven years. Entering the army of the Revolution as lieutenant-colonel, he was colonel in 1777, and in 1782 a brigadier-general. He fought in twenty-two battles. He was afterwards major-general of the militia. From 1797, he was a member of Congress six years. For thirty-four years he was a professor of religion, and a constant attendant upon public worship. His house was a house of prayer. He died at Westfield, Mass., November 11, 1817, aged nearly eighty.—[Allen's *Biog. Dict.*, 3d. edit.]

*She wore a bandage about her breasts, during her disguise, for a very different purpose from that which females wear round their waists. It is not improbable that the severe pressure of this bandage served to compress the bosom, while the waist had every natural convenience for augmentation.

Such is the natural formation and such the appearance of the Female whom I have now introduced into a service dreadful I hope to most men, and certainly destructive to all. Perhaps, exclusive of other irregularities, we must announce the commencement of such an enterprise a great presumption in a female, on account of the inadequateness of her nature. Love and propensity are nearly allied; and we have already discovered the efficacy of both. No love is without hope: but that only is genuine which has for its object virtue, and is attended with resolution and magnanimity. By these the animal economy is enabled to surmount difficulties and to accomplish enterprises and attain objects, which are unattainable by the efforts of the other passions. When love sinks into despondency, the whole system becomes enervated, and is rendered incapacitated for the attainment of common objects. What is Liberty—I mean, in a genuine sense? The love of it prompts to the exposure of our property and the jeopardy of our lives. This is the surest definition of it: For interwoven with and dependent on it, are all our enjoyments. Consequently, love, the noblest passion in man, in no other instance can do more or better show its effects.

CHAPTER VII

March by stages from West Point to Haerlem; from thence to White Plains. Her Company of infantry engage a party of Dutch cavalry. Retreat and are reinforced by Col. Sproat. Capture of the British Army under Lord Cornwallis at Yorktown, where our heroine does duty during the siege.

SIX years having elapsed since our revolutionary Epoch, four years and ten months since our ever memorable Independence—Columbia's Daughter treads the field of Mars![45] And though she might, like Flora, have graced the damask rose,

45 The time when Deborah Sampson joined the army is here declared to have been May, 1781. The same statement is made in the MS. memoir; where, after relating the manner of her leaving home in April, 1781, as she affirms; her visiting Taunton, New Bedford, Boston,

and have continued, peradventure, in the contemplation and un-molested enjoyment of her rural and sylvan scenes; yet for a season she chose the sheathless cutlass and the martial plume.  She is a nymph scarcely past her teens!  Think females, think—but do not resolve till you shall have heard the sequel.

We have already found that she did not engage in this perhaps unprecedented achievement without the precaution of reflection and pathetic debates on the cause.  And this renders her more ex-eusable than many soldiers who rush, like the horse, to the battle, before they establish their proper ultimatum, which is derived only from a thorough investigation of the principles of the contention. Happy for us that a dissemination of this knowledge is oftener the effect of a confederated Republic, than of the jurisdiction of an un-limited monarch.  But neither a delirium, nor love in distraction, has driven her precipitate to this direful extremity.  In cool blood, yet with firm attachment, we now see blended in her the peerless-ness of enterprise, the deportment, ardor and heroism of the veteran, with the milder graces, vigor and bloom of her secreted, softer sex.

Dedham, and other towns; her enlistment at Bellingham, &c.,—she adds, "It was near the last of April when we arrived at Worcester, where a regular muster and enrolment took place
      A large company of us then commenced our march for the camp at West Point, commanded by a sergeant, who was sent from the lines for that purpose." She then describes at considerable length, and in an animated, picturesque style, the march to the Hudson.  "We crossed the Housatonic," she says, "at New Milford, on the 12th of May." A day or two later, they crossed the Hudson at West Point, and joined the army.  These statements are made by Mr. Mann as the mouth-piece of Deborah Sampson.

      Notwithstanding this fulness and particularity of statement, there is much reason to be-lieve that she did not enlist till at least a year later.  In her petition to the General Court in January, 1792, she says she enlisted May 20, 1782.  Capt. Thorp, the muster-master, says she enlisted on that day; the resolve of the General Court makes the same statement; the records of the First Baptist Church in Middleborough say, that, in the spring of 1782, she put on men's clothes, and enlisted as a soldier.  In any ordinary case, such evidence would be decisive.  In the aforesaid petition, she would assuredly make the most of her case.  If she had participated in the campaign which resulted in the triumph at Yorktown, she would have said so.  Her silence proves, in our apprehension, that she did not.  But Mr. Mann desired to make an in-teresting book; and therefore included among the experiences of Deborah Sampson the great campaign of 1781.  This matter has been fully considered in the Introduction.

On the tenth day in the morning, at *reveille*-beat, the company
to which she belonged, with some others, had orders to parade and
march.  They drew four days' provision; which, with her large sack
of clothes and martial apparatus, would have been a burden too
much for females accustomed only to delicate labor.  She left
some of her clothes, performed the march, and use soon became a
second nature.

As the infantry belonged to the rangers, a great part of their
business was scouting; which they followed in places most likely
for success.  In this duty she continued till they arrived at Haerlem; where they continued a few days and then proceeded in like
manner to White Plains.  Here they, in their turn, kept the lines,
and had a number of small skirmishes; but nothing uncommon
occurred in these places.

On July 3d, she experienced in a greater degree, what she had
before mostly known by anticipation.[46]  Captain Webb's com-

46 We know of no reason to doubt the truth of what is related in this paragraph and that
immediately succeeding.  A better statement, abridged from the MS. memoir, with some additions, is the following:—

About the 10th of June, a detachment of troops, including our heroine, received orders to
go out on a scouting-party.  They crossed the Hudson at Stony Point.  This brought them
to the east side of that river.  Their destination was the Neutral Ground between the American
and British armies.  They halted for one night at Tarrytown, where the detachment was divided
into two parties.  They soon came into the vicinity of the enemy's pickets, which they were
careful to elude.  They proceeded as far as Haerlem, within the British lines, and only eight
miles from the city of New York, then held by the British army.  After making such observations of the enemy's positions as they were able, they turned back to the White Plains.  About
the 25th of June, they left the White Plains, and directed their course towards the Hudson.
The next day, the skirmish happened which is related in the text.  It took place in the neighborhood of Tappan Bay, between Sing Sing and Tarrytown.  The party encountered was a detachment from Col. Delancey's regiment of dragoons, consisting chiefly, if not wholly, of Tories,
and then stationed at Morrisania, near the Sound.  This regiment consisted in part of descendants of the old Dutch settlers: hence the phrase in the text, "Dutch cavalry."  Delancey
was an active officer; and his regiment made frequent incursions beyond the British lines, bent
on rapine and often committing acts of great cruelty.

The enemy commenced the attack by a volley from their carbines; then suddenly wheeled
about and galloped away.  The Americans, being on foot, had no opportunity to return the
fire.  Repeating the attack, their second fire was answered by a most deadly discharge from
the Continentals.  The enemy being re-enforced by a party of Tories on foot, the Americans

pany being on a scout in the morning, and headed by Ensign Town, came up with a party of Dutch cavalry from Gen. Delancie's core then in Morsena. They were armed with carabines, or fusees, and broad swords. The action commenced on their side. The Americans withstood two fires before they had orders to retaliate. The ground was then warmly disputed for considerable time. At length the infantry were obliged to give way: but they were quickly reinforced by a detachment led on by Col. Sproat, a valiant officer of the second Massachusetts regiment.[47] They were then too much for the enemy, although a large number had landed from boats for their assistance. The ground they had gained was then measured back with precipitance, even to a considerable distance within their own lines, where the action terminated.

The Americans having retired to their encampment, our fair soldier, with some others, came near losing her life by drinking cold water. She says she underwent more with the fatigue and heat of the day, than by fear of being killed; although her left-hand man was shot dead at the second fire, and her ears and eyes

were compelled to retreat to a piece of woods near by, still keeping up a scattering fire. They were soon strengthened by the arrival of part of Col. Sproat's regiment, and poured in a destructive fire upon the enemy, who were speedily compelled to a hasty and disorderly retreat, after sustaining a heavy loss.

It must have been in this encounter that she was wounded, although "The Female Review" and the MS. memoir represent the wound as having been received in a skirmish with a marauding party of Tories at a later period. Both in her petition to the General Court, January, 1792, and in her declaration under oath, September, 1818, she says she was wounded at Tarrytown.

47 This excellent officer, Col. Ebenezer Sproat, was a native of Middleborough. He was the tallest man in the brigade of Gen. John Glover, of which his regiment formed a part; being six feet and four inches in height. Of the perils of the war he largely partook, being engaged in the battles of Trenton, Princeton, Monmouth, and many others. His superior excellence as a disciplinarian attracted the notice of the Baron Steuben, inspector-general of the army, who appointed him inspector of the brigade. After the war, he was one of the leaders in the enterprise of settling the present State of Ohio; and was known to the Indians as the "Big Buckeye;" whence originated the term since applied to all the people of that State. He died suddenly, at Marietta, his residence, in February, 1805, aged fifty-three.—[Hildreth's *Early Settlers of Ohio.*]

Our author is not careful about his spelling. In the text we have "Gen. Delancie" for Col. Delancey; 'core" instead of corps; and Morrisania is transformed into "Morsena," all in a single line.

were continually tormented with the expiring agonies and horrid scenes of many others struggling in their blood. She recollects but three on her side who were killed, John Beeby, James Battles and Nooble Spern.[48] She escaped with two shots through her coat, and one through her cap.

Perhaps by this time some may be ready to tax her with extreme obduracy, and without mercy to announce her void of all delicacy of sentiment and feeling. And really, had this been her customary plight in her kitchen at home, she might not have passed for an agreeable companion: for she was perfectly besmeared with gunpowder. But if we reflect that this was not the effect of indolence or sluttishness, but for aught we know, of the most endearing attachment to her country, it ought at least to awaken the gratitude of those who may remain too callous to this great philanthropic passion. It behooves every one to consider that war, though to the highest degree destructive and horrid, is effectually calculated to rouze up many tender and sympathetic passions. If the principles of humanity and benevolence are ever to be forced into exertion, war, which should be the last resource, must have the desired effect. And this renders it at best, but a necessary evil; and the promoters of it are the subjects of the greatest aspersion. Let us be free from all other evils, to which dire necessity does not prompt, and we may excuse even a female for taking arms in defence of all that is dear and lovely. She doubtless once thought she could never look on the battle array. She now says no pen can describe her feelings experienced in the commencement of an engagement, the sole object of which is to open the sluices of human blood. The unfeigned tear of humanity has more than once started into her eyes in the rehearsal of such a scene as I have just described.[49]

48 Others were killed and wounded, she knew not how many. These names she happened to remember, as she was well acquainted with the persons. The proper spelling is John Beebe, James Battles, Noble Sperin.

49 At this place she mentions, in the MS. memoir, that, just after this skirmish, she came to be under the command of Col. Henry Jackson, a native of Boston. But Col. Jackson did

From this time till Autumn nothing unusual in war happened to her. Indeed it may be said everything she did in this situation was singular; much of which might afford amusement and moral inferences. But the limits prescribed to these Memoirs will not admit the detail of minute circumstances.[50]

· In August, the Marquis de la Fayette had been dispatched from the main army to contemplate the operations of Lord Cornwallis's army in Virginia. After a multiplicity of military manoeuvres between them, his Lordship selected Yorktown and Gloncester Point as the most conspicuous and advantageous posts for the seat of military operations. Yorktown lies on the river of the

not assume the command of the Fourth Massachusetts Regiment, in which she was a soldier, till some time in 1782, upon the promotion of Col. Shepard, its former commander, to the rank of brigadier-general: so that here is additional evidence that our heroine did not join the army till May, 1782.

In the MS. memoir, in immediate connection with the mention of Col. Jackson, she also says, "In Col. Jackson's regiment I readily recognized Dr. James Thacher of Plymouth, our surgeon. I had before known him at his house and in its vicinity," &c. It appears from Dr. Thacher's "Military Journal," a work of high authority in regard to the Revolutionary War, that he was at this time surgeon of Col. Henry Jackson's regiment. "Col. Henry Jackson, who commands our regiment," he says, "is a native of Boston. He is very respectable as a commander, is gentlemanly in his manners, strongly attached to military affairs, and takes a peculiar pride in the discipline and martial appearance of his regiment." The MS. memoir, from which I have so often quoted, speaks of Col. Jackson in terms of the warmest eulogy. "There was," it says, "an affability and yet a dignity of manner that won the hearts of all under his command. This rendered obedience to orders, and submission to discipline, easy."

Col. Jackson, after the war, resided in Boston, was we believe a brigadier-general in the militia, and had the care of Mrs. Swan's large property while her husband was a prisoner in France. He is represented as having been an elegant and fascinating man. He died in 1809. and his remains were deposited in Mrs. Swan's tomb in Dorchester. He was never married.

50 We now enter on the details of the glorious and decisive campaign of 1781. The various operations included in this campaign are related with much more fulness in the MS. memoir than in this volume. The account extends through eighty pages, equalling in length the previous portion of the memoir. But this account, it is perfectly evident, was not furnished by Deborah Sampson, but was taken by Mr. Mann, the compiler, from the printed accounts of those transactions, especially from Thacher's "Military Journal." This work must have been before him all the while; for he borrows from it constantly, and uses the very words of Dr. Thacher in more than twenty instances; and yet Deborah Sampson is represented as the speaker through the whole. This portion of the MS. memoir is written in a better style than the preceding and subsequent portions, indicating its origin. Dr. Thacher was present at the siege of Yorktown.

same name, which empties into the Chesapeak. It forms a capacious harbor, admitting ships of great burthen. Gloucester Point being on the opposite side, and projecting so far into the river that the distance being but about a mile, they entirely command the navigation of it. Thither Cornwallis with 7,000 excellent troops repaired, strongly fortified the places, and made other good arrangements.

About the last of August Count de Grasse arrived with a powerful French fleet in the Chesapeak, and blockaded Yorktown by water. Soon after, Admiral Graves with a fleet appeared off the capes of Virginia. The French immediately slipped their cables, turned out of their anchorage ground, and an action succeeded; and though both sides sustained considerable loss, it was not decisive.

The Generals Washington and Rochambeau had previously moved their main armies to the southward: and when they heard of the French Admiral's arrival in the Chesapeak they made the most rapid marches till they arrived at the head of the Elk. Within an hour after their arrival they received an express from De Grasse, with the joyful intelligence of his arrival and situation. The combined armies embarked on board the vessels which the French Admiral had previously prepared to transport them down the Chesapeak; and by the 25th of September they landed at Williamsburgh. The American and French Chief Commanders had reached Williamsburgh by excessive travelling eleven days sooner. They immediately proceeded to visit the Admiral on board the *Ville de Paris*. A council being called and their plan of co-operation settled, they returned; and all the Americans and allied troops soon formed a collision at Williamsburgh.[51] Fayette had previously been joined by 3,000 under the Marquis de St. Simon: The whole regular force thus collected amounted to nearly 12,000 men, exclusive of the Virginia militia, which were called

51 "Formed a junction,"—"united their forces," the writer means to say.

to service, and commanded by Governor Nelson. Preparations were then made with great dispatch for putting the army in a situation to move on to Yorktown.

It is almost needless to mention the hardships that common soldiers must have undergone in so long and rapid a march. The deficiency of clothing, particularly of shoes, but most of all, the scanty and wretched quality of provisions, augmented their sufferings. Our heroine sustained her march from some part of New York with good heart, and without faltering, till the day on which she landed with the troops at Williamsburgh. She was then much indisposed; which was not the only time she had experienced the inconveniences of the concealment of her sex. She puked for several hours without much intermission; which she imputed chiefly to the rolling of the vessel. With the rest, she here drew good provision and spirits: and by the next day, she was revived; and the lustre and august manoeuvring of the army seemed to perfect a cure beyond the reach of medicine.

On the morning of the 28th of September, after parade and review, General Orders were read to the armies; wherein his Excellency, Gen. Washington, emphatically enjoined—"If the enemy should be tempted to meet the army on its march, the General particularly enjoins the troops to place their principal reliance on the bayonet, that they may prove the vanity of the boast, which the British make of their peculiar prowess in deciding battles by that weapon." After this, the American and French Chief Commanders personally addressed their armies. Our blooming soldier, always attentive to understand every new manoeuvre and eventful scene, happened to stand so near his Excellency Gen. Washington, that she heard distinctly what he said. He spoke with firm articulation and winning gestures: but his aspect and solemn mode of utterance affectingly bespoke the great weight, that rested on his mind. The common soldiers were before mostly ignorant of the expedition, upon which they were going.[52]  Being now informed by General Orders and the affectionate addresses of their leaders, every countenance, even of many who had discovered a mutinizing spirit, wore an agreeable aspect, and a mutual harmony and reverential acquiescence in the injunctions of their commanders were reciprocated through the whole.

The phalanx composed the advanced guards, and was mostly commanded by De La Fayette.  Our heroine was one of these; and by reason of the absence of a non-commissioned officer, she was appointed to supply his place.  Just before the setting of the sun, Col. Scammell, being officer of the day, brought word for the army to halt two miles from Yorktown.  The officers and soldiers were strictly enjoined to lie on their arms all night.

Such language (strange to say) was perfectly familiar to our fair soldier.  It did not even excite in her a tremor, although it was a prelude to imminent danger.  She had been used to keep her martial apparatus bright and in the best order, as they were often prematurely wanted.  Anticipating no greater danger than she had often actually experienced, although she foreboded a great event, she acquiesced in the mandates of her officers with a calmness that might have surprised an unexperienced soldier.

Next morning, after roll-call, their equipments again reviewed, they went through the quick motions of loading and firing blank cartridges by the motion of the sword.  They formed in close column, displayed* to the right and left, and formed again.  The grand division then displayed, formed by platoon, when they were ordered to march in the best order.  The next day, Col. Scammell, approaching the enemy's works, was mortally wounded and taken prisoner by a party of horse in ambuscade.  Yorktown was this day strongly invested by the allied armies.  Their lines being

*Deployed.

52 No soldier in the American army, after reaching Philadelphia, could have been ignonrat as to the design of the expedition.

formed, the French extending from the river above the town to a morass, where they were met by the Americans on the right, their hard fatigues begun. They continued more than a week laborious, sustaining a very heavy cannonade from the besieged. This business came near proving too much for a female in her teens. Being naturally ambitious, it was mortification too severe for her to be outdone. Many apparently able-bodied men complained they were unfit for duty, and were relieved. Among others, she affected pleasure in giving them the mortifying consolation—that, although she believed their fever was settled upon them, she hoped it would prove nothing worse than the cannon or gunpowder fever.

The fifth night she was one of a party who was ordered to work on a battery, the completion of which had been prevented by a too intense rain of bombs. Before morning she was almost ready to yield to the horrors of despair. Her hands were so blistered that she could scarcely open or shut them: and it was nearly twenty four hours since she had taken much nourishment. But she resolved to persevere as long as nature would make her efforts; which she effected almost beyond credibility.

On the ninth, the American intrenchments being completed, a severe cannonade and bombardment commenced by them on the right, and continued all night without intermission. Next morning, the French opened their redoubts and batteries on the left; and a tremendous roar of cannon and mortars continued that day without ceasing. Our heroine had never before seen either of the main armies together. Being thus brought into view of them and led on to a general engagement, doubtless excited in her sensations and emotions different from what she had before experienced. And I should need the pathos of a Homer, and the polished numbers of a Hume or Pope to do justice to her feelings, or to exceed the reality of this scenery. The ground actually trembled for miles by the tremendous cannonade, which was incessantly maintained by both sides day and night. Notwithstanding it was not so horribly destructive as is generally the consequence of an open field action; yet the contemplation of two immense armies, headed by the most illustrious leaders, each strenuously contending for victory, must have afforded ideas peculiarly shocking and august. The nights exhibited scenes to the highest degree solemn and awfully sublime. Perpetual sheets of fire and smoke belched, as from a volcano, and towered to the clouds. And whilst the eye was dazzled at this, the ear was satiated and stunned by the tremendons explosion of artillery and the screaming of their shot.[53]

I shall here notice a heroic deed of this gallantress; which, while it deserves the applause of every patriot and veteran, must chill the blood of the tender and sensible female.

Two bastion redoubts of the enemy having advanced two hundred yards on the left, which checked the progress of the combined forces, it was proposed to reduce them by storm. To inspire emulation in the troops, the reduction of one was committed to the Americans, and the other to the French. A select corps was chosen. The command of the infantry was given to Fayette, with permission to manage as he pleased. He therefore ordered them to remember Cherry Valley and New London Quarter, and to retaliate accordingly, by putting them to the sword, after having carried the redoubts.[54] Our Heroine was one of these! At dark they marched to the assault with unloaded arms, but with fixed bayonets; and with unexampled bravery, attacking on all sides at once, after some time of violent resistance were complete victors of the redoubts. There were two women in the one attacked by the

[53] The cannonade, on the part of the British, commenced September 27; on the part of the allied army, not till the completion of their trenches, October 9.

[54] There is much reason for doubting the truth of this statement. Dr. Thacher, who gives a particular account of the assault and capture of these two redoubts, makes no allusion to such orders. He says distinctly—"not a man was killed after he ceased to resist." "Such was the order displayed by the assailants, that all resistance was soon overcome." A New Hampshire captain, wishing to avenge the death of Colonel Scammell threatened to take the life of Major Campbell, who commanded the redoubt on the left of the British line; but Col. Alexander Hamilton, who led the storming party, would not suffer it to be done.

Americans, and when our fair soldier entered the third was unknown. After entering the carnage was shocking for a few minutes. She, standing near one of the women, heard her pronounce Yankee,* which was no sooner articulated, than she saw a bayonet plunged into her breast, and the crimson, vital liquid, that gushed from the incision, prevented her further utterance! After this, they cried and begged so on their knees for quarter, that the humanity of the Americans overcame all resentment, and they spared all who ceased to resist; for which they were afterwards applauded by their humane officers. Before they left the fort, one clapped her on the shoulder, and said—"Friend, fear not; you are only disfigured behind." She took no apparent notice of what he said, till an opportunity presented: when, happy for her, she found it no worse! The lapelle of her coat dangled by string; which must have been the effect of a broad sword, or of a very close shot.[56]

Was not this enterprise, alone, in a female, worth the attainment of liberty? Yet, where is the fair one who could again hazard it! Methinks I see the crimson cheek of the female turning pallid, her vigorous limbs relaxing and tottering in the rehearsal of this eventful scene. Yet, let no one imagine I have painted it to the life. The fact is simply narrated; and the proper

*The derivation of this word is from farmer Jonathan Hastings of Cambridge about 1713. He used it to express a good quality. Thus, a yankee horse and yankee cider, were an excellent horse and excellent cider.[55]—The British used it wrongly, as a word of contempt to the Americans. Thus, when they marched out of Boston in 1775, they played a march, called Yankee Doodle; though the prediction of an active boy was—that their retrograde march would be to Chevy Chase. During this siege, two bombs having fell, their fuses were extracted whilst burning; one by a Female, the other by a Soldier. The contents of one were squash, of the other, molasses.

55 This account of the derivation of the word "Yankee" is borrowed from Thacher's "Military Journal," p. 19. It is, nevertheless, wholly unsatisfactory. The more probable derivation is from the word "English," corrupted by the Indians into Yenglees, then Yanklees, and finally Yankees.

56 Was Deborah Sampson here at this time? Did she work in the trenches, with blistered hands, on the night of the 7th October? Was she one of the storming-party on the night of the 15th? Did she witness the surrender of Cornwallis? We confess we have our doubts on the subject.

coloring is left for those peculiar inmates of the female benevolent
and heroic breasts.   I hasten to drop the scene.

The French commanders, whose services demand the grati
tude of every American, led on their troops with a heroic bravery,
scarcely to be excelled.   And whilst De Grasse displayed much
valor, and was doing great execution with his Armada, the Americans, headed by the ever dear and unrivalled Washington redoubled
their activity and resolution.   Nothing thus but inevitable ruin,
or an entire surrender, awaited Cornwallis and on then 19th of
October, after three weeks' severe storm,[57] an armistice having
taken place for twenty-four hours, he was glad to accept the terms
of capitulation.   He was not permitted to march out with colors
flying—an honor that had been refused to Gen. Lincoln the preceding winter, when he, with all the American garrison, was captured in Charleston, South Carolina,[58]   Lincoln was now appoint
ed to receive his sword and the submission of the royal army precisely in the mode his own had been conducted.

The marching out of such an immense army, as prisoners of
war, must have been a scene the most solemn and important.
The magnanimity which was discovered in Gen. Washington upon
this occasion, was inexpressibly peculiar.   Tears trickled from his
eyes during the most of the scene.[59]   And a view of him in these
moments must have forced a tear of reverential gratitude from the
most obdurate.   He thought of his Country!—Remember the
Patriot—remember the Philanthropist!

57  The allied forces, about 12,000 strong, arrived before Yorktown September 27.   They
were engaged till October 9 in throwing up intrenchments; suffering all the while a severe cannonade from the town.   On the evening of the 9th they first opened fire on the British lines.

58  Gen. Lincoln with his army, and the city of Charleston, surrendered to the British
forces under Sir Henry Clinton, May 12, 1780.

59  Gen. Washington was not inclined to weep, and it is not likely that he wept on this
occasion.   Dr. Thacher, who was an eye-witness of the scene, and describes it with great par-
ticularity, makes no mention of such want of self-control on the part of the American commander-in-chief.

Thus was the grand pillar of war at length broken down, and an ample foundation laid for the establishment of the so much celebrated and wished for palladium of peace. We certainly owe this event, at least, in a great measure to our generous auxiliaries. Had they not lent us their powerful and timely aid, America, for anything we can tell, might have still clanked her chain under a monarchical and despotic sway. Must not a remembrance of their Leaders, particularly of Fayette, start the tear of gratitude, and of filial and sympathetic attachment? He generously and nobly made Columbia's Cause his own. Unhappy man! Happy perhaps he might have continued, had not his philanthropic designs been baffled in his exertions to put them in execution in his native country. Disappointed in these, his warmest wishes, behold him dragging out a more useful intended existence in a loathsome dungeon!* O wretched, inhuman return for philanthropy—the best services of man!

> See vegetable nature all conspire
> To make man blest, his ultimate desire:
> Yet, mark how erring to great nature's plan,
> That man, made wise, should be unjust to man!

Whilst our blood can never cease to thrill with indignation for his

*Soon after the revolution in France, an accusation was decreed against him; and in attempting to escape, he was apprehended in Magdeburg and imprisoned. Heaven grant, he may have been liberated before this time![60]

60 On the memorable 10th of August, 1792, the populace of Paris rose in arms, attacked the Palace of the Tuileries, massacred the Swiss guards, and dethroned the king. Lafayette, who, during the earlier part of the French Revolution, had concurred in the constitutional reforms decreed by the National Assembly, and who was at this time in command of an army stationed on the frontiers to oppose the Prussian invasion, now felt his own life to be in peril from popular violence. He was, indeed, at this juncture, accused of treason by the popular leaders, and a price was set upon his head. He therefore, on the 17th of August, quitted the army and the territory of France with twelve officers of rank, intending to proceed to the United States. They had travelled but a short distance, when they were all taken prisoners by the Prussians; and Lafayette was put in close confinement in the castle of Magdeburg, once the abode of Baron Trenck, and was soon after imprisoned in the strong fortress of Olmutz. To the honor of Napoleon it should be said that one of the articles of the Treaty of Campo Formio, October 18, 1797, negotiated under the pressure of that conqueror's great successes in Italy, stipulated for the release of Lafayette, after Washington had interceded for him in vain.

sufferings, may our gratitude and reverence never cool towards this illustrious but distressed nobleman. May a reciprocity of friendship and affection conciliate and cement us more strongly with France, our once helpful and now sister republic. We solicit England to shake hands with Columbia, her natural offspring. Let the banners of war be forever furled, the sword of contention sheathed in its proper place; and may she always forget to prove inimical to her established Cause. May philanthropy become as extensive as the nations of the earth. Men shall then quite their fallacious pursuits, retire to their respective and proper occupations, and learn humility and propriety of conduct. Then shall mutual harmony, peace and prosperity pervade the world.

I shall leave our fair Soldier, or as she was frequently called, the blooming boy, in winter quarters not far from West Point and the banks of the Hudson, or North River, in what were called the York huts. She arrived at this place in December, much debilitated and dispirited by hard marches and fatigues. She was destitute of shoes, as were most of the soldiers during the march; excepting raw hides, which they cut into straps and fastened about their feet. It was not uncommon to track them by the bleeding of their feet on the snow and ice.[61] And it appeared, their officers fared not much better; although they used their greatest efforts to soothe, animate and encourage the soldiers, principally with the prospects of peace and the great honor they should gain by persevering to the end.

Just before their arrival, one of her company having been severely chastised for stealing poultry, importuned her to desert with him and two others. But she not only disdainfully refused, but used all the eloquence of which she was mistress, to dissuade them from so presumptive an attempt. Having hazarded one desperate presumption herself, she chose to take her lot in the

61 There is nothing of this sort in the MS. memoir, nor in Thacher's "Military Journal." Of course, there is exaggeration here.

present and future ills; though peradventure her sex might in some measure have justified her breach of contract.  The arguments she enforced were—that it would not only be an evidence of disloyalty to their country, a token of cowardice, a breach of civil obligation, but the greatest jeopardy of their lives.  As female eloquence is generally irresistible, they here yielded to its energy: although they were insensible that it was articulated through female organs.

Having repaired the huts, in which business she froze her feet to that degree that she lost all her toe-nails, the soldiers were culled, in order that all who had not had the small-pox might be inoculated. The soldiers who were to be inoculated, paraded; when our heroine for the first time, shewed an aversion to it.   Determined to hazard taking this malignant distemper unaware, she would even have falsified the truth of her having had it, sooner than have gone to the hospital; where the pride and glory of her sex, the source of the blooming boy, might have been disclosed.[62]

She did duty, sometimes as a common soldier and sometimes as a serjeant; which was mostly on the lines, patrolling, collecting fuel, &c.   As the winter was very intense, the snow the most of the time deep, I shall leave it for the considerate to imagine the unusual hardships of a female in this situation.  She went cheerful to her tasks, and was never found loitering when sent on duty or enter-prize.

62 In the MS. memoir, she says, "Dreading the exposure of my person, and the consequent discovery of my sex, far more than death, I told a plump lie to the surgeon, in the statement that I had long since experienced that disease.   I preferred to hazard taking the small-pox rather than go to the hospital.   I was therefore excused, and by the favor of a kind Providence escaped the contagion, though often exposed to it."

Dr. Thacher places the inoculation of the troops for small-pox in January, 1782.  Of course, it took place before her enlistment.   He inoculated, he says, about two hundred, including women and children.

## CHAPTER VIII

Building of the colonnade on West Point after the opening of the Campaign.   Writes to
her mother.   A severe skirmish, where she receives two wounds, and is left in the
French hospital.   Returns to the army on their lines.   Is left with a sick soldier in
a Dutchman's family, who is a Tory and treats her ill.   Heroic adventure in her
mode of Retaliation.   She and a party, being attacked by a party of Dutch Cavalry,
are obliged to ford a dangerous ferry.   The main Army retire to Winter Quarters
at New Windsor.   She is one of a detachment sent to reinforce Gen. Schuyler in subduing the Indians on the Frontiers above Albany; where a number of horrid scenes
are exhibited.

HAVING now furnished a clue by which the succeeding common occurrences of our distinguished Fair, whilst a soldier, may be gathered, I shall not tire the patience of the reader in their enumeration.   Though, as common as they then were to her, could they be exhibited afresh by an indifferent female, I am confident I have not a reader but would think his leisure interims luxuriantly employed in their recital.   But I hasten to a narration of those on which to dwell must be luxury and wonder; but to pass them unnoticed, criminal injustice.

Though peace had not longer been anticipated than wished for, yet the conduct of both armies after the opening of the campaign seemed to place it as a matter of extreme uncertainty.   The opening of this campaign was distinguished by the building of a Colonnade, or rather a Bowery, on West Point.   It was begun on the 2d of May, and completed after about three weeks' fatigue. In this business our heroic Female often worked against the most robust and expert soldier: and had not the delicate texture of her frame been concealed, it would doubtless have been judged that she was very unequally mated.

When this delightful building was finished, the officers held a meeting of social intercourse and conviviality.   The full, sparkling bowl was here handed cheerfully round.   Many toasts of health and long life were drank to the half-divine Washington— to the true sons of freedom and republicanism—to the increase and perpetuity of our alliance with France, and giving three cheers for the newborn Dauphin of that realm, they concluded the day.[63]

The reader has long enough been in suspense to know what effect her elopement had on her mother and connections, and what method she took to pacify, as we may suppose, their half distracted minds. Though she received her education in obscurity, the news of her elopement, or among other conjectures, that she had come to some untimely catastrophe, flew to a great distance. Her mother, raising a thousand doubts and fears was almost inconsolably wretched. Sometimes she harbored the too often poignant reflection, that her too rigorous exertions to precipitate her union with the gentleman I have before mentioned had driven her to some direful and fatal alternative. The like dire, alternate thoughts filled her undissembled lover with emotions he could ill conceal. And like a man of sense and breeding he commiserated each of their misfortunes. Frantic at times, when reflection had pictured to his imagination all her frightful groups of ideas and images, he would curse his too overbearing importunity and too open declaration of his passions. These, he too late surmised, were the cause of her leaving him abruptly (which, by the bye, is the reverse of common circumstances), and for aught he knew of her casual exit from all earthly objects; or, that the too warm pressure of his love had rendered him odious, and that she had too justly punished

63 Dr. Thacher notices the erection of this edifice, and the magnificent festival in it after it was finished. The festival was on the 31st of May, 1782. About one thousand men were employed about ten days in the construction of this curious edifice, under the direction of Major Villefranche, an ingenious French engineer. It was on the esplanade of West Point, and was composed of the simple materials which the common trees of that vicinity afforded. It was six hundred feet in length, and thirty in width, supported by a grand colonnade of one hundred and eighteen pillars made of the trunks of trees. The roof consisted of branches of trees curiously interwoven, and the walls were of the same materials, leaving the ends entirely open. "This superb structure," he says, "in symmetry of proportion, neatness of workmanship, and elegance of arrangement, has seldom, perhaps, been surpassed on any temporary occasion." The festival held in this remarkable edifice was in honor of the new-born Dauphin of France and of the French alliance. The MS. memoir, from which I have often quoted, describes the edifice and the festival in exact accordance with the account given by Dr. Thacher; in no less than twelve instances, using his very words. Of course, this could not be by mere accident.

him by throwing herself into the embraces of a more agreeable rival. He determined however, were it practicable, once more to see her, and to congratulate her on her union with a better companion than he could make; or, should she conceive as he once thought she had, a growing affection for him, he should rejoice to find himself in the road for that happiness which alone could render his existence satisfactory, or scarcely desirable.

For this purpose one of her brothers made a fruitless expedition a number of hundred miles to the Eastward among some of her relations.[64]  Her suitor took his route to the westward, and among his rambles, he visited the seat of war; where he saw his half adorable object of love.  But as fortune, adverse or propitious, would have it, he knew not that she who appeared in martial attire was the tender object who occupied the most distinguished seat in his bosom.  Her eyes were not deceptory; and when she heard the articulation of her name in his enquiries, it was not because she slighted him, nor because she was enraptured with his love, that she a second time hastened from his presence.  The big tear trembled in her eye, and when she turned to conceal her emotions, she silently and reluctantly bid him adieu.[65]

After many wearisome steps and unsuccessful researches, he returned home; when it was concluded that she must have crossed the wide Atlantic, or have found an untimely sepulchre in her own country.  She was preserved; and she only could cure the cruel suspense and racking sensations which [it] would be brutal to suppose

64 This brother went to Meduncook, now Friendship, on the seacoast of Maine, to see if she had not taken up a residence there with the children of Joshua Bradford, who had married her mother's eldest sister, Hannah Bradford.  See note, page 37.  This place is a few miles west of Penobscot Bay.

65 The account here given is not accurate.  Deborah saw him: it is not certain that he saw her.  Some of her comrades told her of the inquiries he was making respecting her.  By this means, also, she actually heard from home; heard that her mother and other friends were well; that a great excitement had been occasioned by her elopement.  She says she felt tenderly towards him, and would gladly have thanked him for his interest in her welfare; but she did not speak to him, and would not risk a discovery of herself to him.  He therefore returned without success.

did not pervade their bosoms on this occasion. The mind is scarcely capable of picturing a contrast more trying to the tender passions than this. And no doubt, she allotted her sequestered retirements to indulge the sorrowing, unnoticed tear; when the anguish of a mother, of her relatives and of him whose felicity she knew was perfectly interwoven with her own, took complete possession of her mind together. After striving a long time in vain to ease the distress of her mother, and to exonerate the too intense burden of her own mind by writing, she found an opportunity, and enclosed to her the substance of the following:[66]

May, 1782.
Dear Parent,

On the margin of one of those rivers, which intersects and winds itself so beautifully majestic through a vast extent of territory of the United States, is the present situation of your unworthy, but constant and affectionate daughter. I pretend not to justify, or even to palliate my clandestine elopement. In hopes of pacifying your mind, which I am sure must be afflicted beyond measure, I write you this scrawl. Conscious of not having thus abruptly absconded by reason of any fancied ill treatment from you, or disaffection towards any, the thoughts of my disobedience are truly poignant. Neither have I a plea that the insults of man have driven me hence: And let this be your consoling reflection—that I have not fled to offer more daring insults to them by a proffered prostitution of that virtue which I have always been taught to preserve and revere. The motive is truly important; and when I divulge it, my sole ambition and delight shall be to make an expiatory sacrifice for my transgression.

I am in a large, but well regulated family. My employment is agreeable, although it is somewhat different and more intense

66 This letter was doubtless composed, like some of Cicero's orations, long after the time when it was said to have been written. It is given in the MS. memoir with considerable variation in the words, and in a more ambitious style. It is the composition of Mr. Mann, not of Deborah Sampson. The style differs not at all from that of the rest of the book.

than it was at home: But I apprehend it is equally as advantageous. My superintendents are indulgent; but to a punctilio, they demand a due observance of decorum and propriety of conduct. By this you must know, that I have become mistress of many useful lessons, though I have many more to learn. Be not too much troubled, therefore, about my present or future engagements; as I will endeavor to make that prudence and virtue my model for which, I own, I am much indebted to those who took the charge of my youth.

My place of residence and the adjacent country are beyond description delightsome. The earth is now pregnant with vegetation; and the banks of the river are already decorated with all the luxuriance of May. The cottages that peep over the rising grounds seem perched like eagles' nests; and the nobler buildings, well cultivated plantations and the continual passing and re-passing of vessels in the river below, form one of the most pleasingly variegated and noble prospects, I may say, in the world. Indeed were it not for the ravages of war, of which I have seen more here than in Massachusetts, this part of our great continent would become a paradisaical elysium. Heaven condescend that a speedy peace may constitute us a happy and independent nation: when the husband shall again be restored to his amiable consort, to wipe her sorrowing tear, the son to the embraces of his mourning parents and the lover to the tender, disconsolate and half distracted object of his love.—

Your affectionate
DAUGHTER.

This letter, being intrusted with a stranger, was intercepted. Let us now resume her progress in war.

Passing over many marches, forward and retrograde, and numberless incidental adventures and hardships peculiar to war, I come to other Memoirs, which must forcibly touch the passions of every bosom that is not callous to reflection and tenderness of feeling.

The business of war is devastation, rapine and murder.    And
in America, these brutal principles were never more horribly exemplified than in this war.    Hence the necessity of scouting; which was
the common business of the infantry, to which our heroine belonged.
And some time in June of this year, she, with two sergeants, requested leave of their Captain to retaliate on the enemy, chiefly
refugees and Tories in New York for their outrageous insults to
the inhabitants beyond their lines.    He replied—You three dogs
have contrived a plan this night to be killed, and I have no men to
lose."    He however consented; and they beat for volunteers.
Nearly all the company turned out; but only twenty were permitted to go.[67]—Near the close of the day they commenced their expedition.    They passed a number of guards and went as far as
East Chester undiscovered; where they lay in ambush to watch
the motions of those who might be on the plundering business.
They quickly discovered that two parties had gone out; and whilst
they were contriving how to entrap them, they discovered two
boys, who were sent for provisions to a private cellar in the wood.
One of them informed that a party had just been at his mother's,
and were then gone to visit the Yankees, who were guarding the
lines.    Concealing from them that they were Americans, they accompanied them to the cellar, or rather a cave, which they found
well stored. with provision, such as bacon, butter, cheese, crouts,
early scrohons and jars of honey.    They made a delicious repast,
filled their sacks and informed the boys they were Yankees; upon
which the cave loudly rung with their cries.    Dividing into two
parties, they set out centinels and again ambushed in place called
in  Dutch, *Vonhoite.*

About four in the morning, a large party, chiefly on horseback
and well armed, were saluted by one of the centinels; which was no
sooner done than they returned a number of pistol and fusee shots

67 The MS. memoir says about thirty were permitted to go, and that they belonged to
three different companies.    East Chester is four miles east of the Hudson.    Tories were numerous thereabouts.

at the flash of his gun.[68]   A severe combat ensued.   The Americans found horses without riders: they had then light-horse and foot. Our Gallantress having previously become a good horseman, immediately mounted an excellent horse.   They pursued the enemy till they came to a quagmire, as it appeared by their being put to a nonplus.   They rushed on them on the right and left, till as many as could escaped; the rest begged quarter.   The dauntless Fair at this instant thought she felt something warmer than sweat run down her neck.   Putting her hand to the place, she found the blood gushed from the left side of her head very freely.   She said nothing, as she thought it no time to tell of wounds, unless mortal.   Coming to a stand she dismounted, but had not strength to walk, or stand alone.   She found her boot on her right leg filled with blood;[69] and in her thigh, just below her groin, she found the incision of a ball, whence it issued.—Females! this effusion was from the veins of your tender sex, in quest of that Liberty you now so serenely possess.

She told one of the sergeants she was so wounded she chose rather to be left in that horrid place, than be carried any further. They all, as one, concluded to carry her in case she could not ride. Here was her trial!   A thousand thoughts and spectres at once darted before her.   She had always thought she should rather die than disclose her sex to the army!   And at that instant, almost in despair, she drew a pistol from a holster, and was nearly ready to execute the fatal deed.   But divine goodness here stayed her hand:

68 About two in the morning, according to the MS. memoir.   The sentinel was stationed by the party to which our heroine belonged, to give notice of the approach of the party of refugees, who, according to the information obtained from the boy, were expected soon to repair to the dépôt of provisions.   The sentinel gave notice by firing his gun; upon which, Deborah's party fired at the party of refugees, killing several, and putting the others to flight, after a short but severe struggle.

69 The left leg, according to the MS. memoir.   This shows that our author was not accurate in matters of detail.

and the shocking act and idea of suicide were soon banished by her cooler reason.[70]

Having rested a little, being destitute of any refreshment, her wounds became excessively painful; but nothing we may judge, to the anguish of her mind. Coming in view at length of the French encampment, near what was called Cron Pond, she says, it was to her like being carried reluctant to the place of execution.

[70] "I considered this as a death-wound, or as being equivalent to it; as it must, I thought, lead to the discovery of my sex. Covered with blood from head to foot, I told my companions I feared I had received a mortal wound; and I begged them to leave me to die on the spot; preferring to take the small chance I should in this case have of surviving, rather than to be carried to the hospital. To this my comrades would not consent; but one of them took me before him on his horse, and in this painful manner I was borne six miles to the hospital of the French army, at a place called Croon Pond.* On coming in sight of the hospital, my heart again failed me. In a paroxysm of despair, I actually drew a pistol from the holster, and was about to put an end to my own life. That I did not proceed to the fatal act, I can ascribe only to the interposition of Divine Mercy.

The French surgeon, on my being brought in, instantly came. He was alert, cheerful, humane. 'How you lose so much blood at dis early hour? Be any bone broken?' was his first salutation; presenting me and the other wounded men of our party with two bottles of choice wine . . . . My head having been bound up, and a change of clothing becoming a wounded soldier being ready, I was asked by the too inquisitive French surgeon whether I had any other wound. He had observed my extreme paleness, and that I limped in attempting to walk. I readily replied in the negative: it was a plump falsehood! 'Sit you down, my lad— your boot say you tell fib!' said the surgeon, noticing that the blood still oozed from it. He took off my boots and stocking with his own hands with great tenderness, and washed my leg to the knee. I then told him I would retire, change my clothing, and if any other wound should appear, I would inform him.

Meanwhile I had procured in the hospital a silver probe a little curved at the end, a needle, some lint, a bandage, and some of the same kind of salve that had been applied to the wound in my head. I found that the ball had penetrated my thigh about two inches, and the wound was still moderately bleeding. The wine had revived me, and God, by his kind care, watched over me. At the third attempt, I extracted the ball, which, as a sacred relic, I still possess.†

This operation over, the blood was stanched, and my regimentals, stiff enough with blood to stand alone, had been exchanged for a loose, thin wrapper, when I was again visited by the surgeon. In his watchful eye I plainly read doubts. I told him that all was well; that I felt much revived, and wished to sleep. I had slept scarcely an hour, when he again alarmed me. Approaching me on my mattress of straw, and holding my breeches in his hand, dripping from

*Crom Pond, east of Peekskill.

†In the Report of the Committee of Congress, January 31, 1837 (see Introduction, page xxi.), it is stated that the ball was never extracted, and "that the effect of the wound continued through life, and probably hastened her death."

‥

They were conducted by the officer of the guards to an old hospital, in which was a number of soldiers, whose very looks, she says, were enough to make a well man indisposed, and the nauseous smell to infect the most pure air.  The French surgeon soon came; who, being informed of their circumstances, gave them two bottles of choice wine, and prepared to dress their wounds.  His mate, washing her head with rum, told her, he supposed it had not come to its feeling, as she did not flinch.  Judge, my readers, whether this was not the case, as her other wound so much affected her heart!

the wash-tub, 'How came this rent?' said he, putting his finger into it.  I replied, 'It was occasioned, I believe, on horseback, by a nail in the saddle or holster.  'Tis of no consequence. Sleep refreshes me: I had none last night.'  One-half of this, certainly, was true.  But I had less dread of receiving half a dozen more balls than the penetrating glance of his eye.  As I grew better, his scrutiny diminished.

Before the wound in my thigh was half healed, I rejoined the army on the lines.  But had the most hardy soldier been in the condition I was when I left the hospital, he would have been excused from military duty."—[MS. Memoir.]

There is no doubt that she was wounded, as now related; for it is stated in her petition to the Legislature, and in other authentic memorials.  But her petition and her declaration say that she was wounded at Tarrytown, which place is not mentioned in the foregoing account. This account locates the skirmish at or near East Chester, four or five miles east of the Hudson; whereas Tarrytown is situated on that river.  The encounter with a party of Delancey's dragoons, related a few pages back, was therefore the occasion when she was wounded; and the *Female Review* is here, as in many other places, inaccurate.

Mrs. Ellet says, "She was a volunteer in several hazardous enterprises; the first time by a sword-cut on the left side of the head."  This must have been in the cavalry encounter at Tarrytown.  "About four months after her first wound, she received another severe one, being shot through the shoulder.  Her first emotion when the ball entered she described to be a sickening terror at the probability that her sex would be discovered.  She felt that death on the battlefield were preferable to the shame that would overwhelm her, and ardently prayed that the wound might close her earthly campaign.

Many were the adventures she passed through: as she herself would often say, volumes might be filled with them.  Sometimes placed unavoidably in circumstances in which she feared detection, she nevertheless escaped all suspicion.  The soldiers were in the habit of calling her "Molly," in playful allusion to her want of a beard; but not one of them ever dreamed that the gallant youth fighting by their side was in reality a female."—[*Women of the Revolution*].

Mrs. Ellet had never seen the *Female Review*, but received her information "from a lady who knew her personally, and had often listened with thrilling interest to the animated description given by herself of her exploits and adventures."  Yet some of Mrs. Ellet's details are unreliable.

She requested the favor of more medicine than she needed for her head; and taking an opportunity, with a penknife and needle, she extracted the ball from her thigh; which, by that time, had doubtless come to its feeling.

They never rightly knew how many they killed or wounded. They took nine prisoners and seven horses, and killed a number of others on the spot. Of their wounded was Rose, Stockbridge, Plummer and the invincible Fair. Diston was killed.

After suffering almost every pain but death, with incredible fortitude, she so far healed her wound unbeknown to any, that she again joined the army on the lines. But its imperfect cure, had it been known, would have been sufficient to exempt the most hardy soldier from duty.

In August, on their march to the lines from Collabarack,* she requested to be left with a sick soldier named Richard Snow; mostly because she was unable to do duty with the army, and partly out of compassion for the poor object, who was sick.[71] But the fortune of war to her proved adverse. The fears and distress that here awaited her, were far greater than those when with the army. The old Dutchman, whose name was Van Tassel, with whom she was left, was not only a Tory and entertained the banditti, who plundered the Americans, but refused them all kinds of succor. When she begged a straw bed for the expiring soldier, he virulently exulted—"The floor is good enough for rebels." They were lodged in a dirty garret without windows; where the heat rendered it still more insupportable.

*Probably Claverack in the present Columbia County.

71 "About a fortnight after I rejoined my company, I obtained permission to stay and nurse a sick soldier, whose name was Richard Snow, at a place called Collebarack. Opportunity was thus afforded not only for the exercise of humanity to a distressed comrade, but for the more speedy cure of my wound, which the duties of the camp would not allow to be perfectly healed."—[MS. Memoir.]

It never was perfectly healed.

One night, expecting to become a prey to the relentless cruelty
of the rabble, she charged both their pieces, resolving to sacrifice
the first who might offer to molest.[72]   She likewise made fast a rope
near an opening in the garret, by which to make her escape, in
case they should be too many.   Thus she continued  constant to
him, till almost exhausted for want of sleep and nourishment.   On
the tenth night, he expired in great agonies, but in the exercise of
his reason (of which he was before deprived), and much resigned
to the will of God; which may be a consolation to his surviving relatives.

After Snow was dead, she rolled him in his blanket and sat
at the avenue.[73]   She saw a party ride up to the house, and the old
churl go out to congratulate them.   They informed, the horses they
then had, with other plunder, were taken from the Americans.
Whilst the house was again infested with their ungodly career, it is
not in my power to describe her melancholy distress in a dark garret
with a corpse.   A multitude of cats swarmed in the room; and it
was with difficulty she disabled some with her cutlass, and kept
the rest from tearing the body to pieces.   At length she heard foot-
steps on the stairs.   Her heart fluttered; but her heroism had  not
forsaken her.   Hastening to the door, she put her hanger in a position to dislocate the limbs of any who should enter.   But the
voice of a female, who spoke to her in English, allayed her fear.
It was Van Tassel's daughter, who seemed possessed of  humanity,
and who had before often alleviated her distress.

At daybreak, she left the garret; but finding the  outer  doors
bolted, she was returning, when she again met the young female,
who bid her good morning, and said—"If you please, Sir, walk into
my chamber."   She followed; and seating themselves by a window,

72 "The rabble" means the Tories, who resorted to the house, and were at the time in the
lower part of the house, revelling in the spoil they had taken from honest people in the vicinity.
"Both their pieces,"—her gun and the sick soldier's.

73 "After Snow was dead, I wrapped him in his blanket, and seated myself at the open
window to inhale fresh air."

they regaled themselves with a glass of wine and a beautiful, serene air. After entreating her agreeable guest not to let the ill treatment she had received from her father make her forsake the house, she bordered on subjects that might have enraptured the other sex.[74]—Summoned at this instant by her mother, they withdrew.

Our heroine, with the assistance of two others, buried the dead; then sat out to join her company. She acquainted the Captain of the toryism of Van Tassel, of his treatment of her, and thought it best to surprise him. The affair was submitted to her management. She frequented the house; and having learned that a gang was to be there at such a time, she took command of a party and found them in their usual reverie.[75] Some thought best to rush immediately upon them; but she deemed it more prudent to wait till their intoxicated brains should render them less capable of resistance. At midnight she unbolted the stable doors, when they possessed themselves of the horses; then rallied the house. They came out with consternation, which was increased when they were told, they were dead men if they did not yield themselves prisoners of war. They conveyed them to their company as such.[76] The Captain enquired of the gallant Commander, the method of capturing them; which she detailed. He gave her a bottle of good spirits and told her to treat her men. This done, she requested that the prisoners might fare in like manner. The Captain said— "Will you treat men who would be glad to murder us?" But she pleading the cause of humanity, he gave her another bottle. Unlosing the hands of a sergeant, he drank but in making them fast

74 Instead of the clause, "she bordered on subjects," &c., the MS. memoir has, "I replied that her father would soon be obliged to leave his house, and his country took uuless he changed his course. She spoke strongly against her father's Toryism, from which she herself had often suffered."

75 For "reverie" read "revelry." The meaning is, the tories were rioting on the plunder they had taken.

76 Without shedding any blood, our heroine's party captured fifteen Tories and nine horses, and brought them safely to camp. The MS. memoir spreads this affair over six pages.

again, he acted on the defensive, and struck her to the ground. She arose, when he made a second attempt; but she warded the blow. His compeers chided him for his folly, as they had been well used. He vented many bitter oaths; alleging, she had not only taken him prisoner, but had caused his girl (meaning Van Tassel's daughter) to pay that attention to her she once bestowed on him. He, however, received fifty stripes on the naked back for his insolence; then was sent to Headquarters, and after trial, to the Provost, with the rest at West Point.

The beginning of Autumn she, with Lieut. Brown and others, had a boisterous cruise down the Hudson to Albany on business;[77] soon after, a scouting tour into the Jersies; and she was with the armies on the 19th of October in their grand Display at Virplank's Point.[78] I only instance these as parties of pleasure and a day of jubilee, when compared with the rougher events of war.[79]

We come now to the first of December, when she and a party were surprised by a party of Dutch cavalry from an ambuscade and drove with impetuosty to Croton Ferry; where their only alternative was that of fording it or of risking their lives with the assailants: each of which seemed to the last degree dangerous. Without time for hesitation, compelling a Dutchman to pilot them on the bar, they entered the watery element; and by the assistance

77 They could not go "down the Hudson" from West Point to Albany.

78 About the middle of September, there was a grand display of the army at King's Ferry, on account of the return of Count Rochambeau from the South."—[MS. Memoir.]

This review is noticed by Dr. Thacher in his "Military Journal." It was on the 14th of September, 1782. As usual, the compiler of the MS. memoir borrows some of Thacher's expressions.

79 On the former of these occasions, the scouting-party, or raid, as it would now be called, went out to capture Tories, an employment in which our heroine delighted. She considered them, as they really were, by far the worst enemies of the country. Never did a hunter in pursuit of game, with the pack in full cry, feel better than did she when in pursuit of Tories. She says, "I loved to watch by these Tories, and to steal away their dreams. And yet in no part of my military career have I been more exposed to danger. On this occasion we had little success, these freebooters having mostly taken refuge within the British lines." This expedition was chiefly in New Jersey.

of that Being who is said to have conducted the Israelites through the Red Sea, they reached the other shore.[80]

They went to the house of the Widow Hunt; who, under pretentions of friendship, sent black George for refreshment.[81] But our heroine, more acquainted with the cunning of her sex, advised them not to adhere to her smoothness of speech. Accordingly, they went back to the ferry; and they can best describe the wretchedness of their situation during a cold winter night. In the morning, though the river was frozen, they determined to recross it, lest the enemy should drive them to a worse extremity. Before they had two-thirds crossed, the strength of our young Female was so exhausted that the briskness of the stream, which was in height to her chin, carried her off the bar; when it was concluded, she was for ever ingulphed in a watery tomb. As she rose, summoning the last exertions of nature, she got hold of a string, which they buoyed to her; and thus providentially regained the bar and shore. Frozen and languid as they then were, they reached a store; where not being well used, they burst in the head of a brandy cask, drank their fill, gave a shoe-full to the negro of the widow, whom they had before taken; then left him in a better situation than he said his mistress meant to have left them. She rendezvoused with her company at Pixhill Hollow.[82]

80 "In the second of these expeditions, about the 1st of December," says the MS. memoir, —though it could not have been later than early in November,—"We fell into an ambuscade formed by the enemy's cavalry. Endeavoring to escape, we had no alternative but to ford Croton River, or risk an engagement with treble our number. We chose to ford the river; and, compelling a Dutchman to conduct us to a place where the water was but breast high, we reached the opposite shore in safety." Our heroine's party were on foot.

81 "We went to the house of a Widow Hunt, who proved to be a desperate female Tory. She sent her slave, black George, ostensibly for refreshments, but really to give information to the enemy, the party whom we had just escaped. During that cold winter night, we were without shelter, and my wound not yet perfectly healed." They had just forded the river. Of course, their clothes were drenched with the water, which froze upon them. "Before we had recrossed the river a large body of the enemy appeared in pursuit," etc.

82 This should be, as in the MS. memoir, "Peekskill Hollow." This was a noted military post on the Hudson in the Revolutionary War.

Soon after the army retired to Winter Quarters at New Windsor, the clarion of war was again sounded for a reinforcement to assist Gen. Schuyler in subduing the Indians on the frontiers, on to Saratoga.[83]  The officers chose to form their detachment of volunteers; as the soldiers were worn down with the hardships of war. Heavens! what will not resolution and perseverance surmount, even in the fair sex!—Our heroine offered her service; though an inflammation of her wound would have deterred a veteran: it being an open sore a few days before she crossed the river.[84]

Their marches were over the ruins of Indian barbarity.  On their return they flanked into parties, and took different routes

[83] According to Thacher's "Military Journal," the left wing of the army, under Gen. Heath, after a march from Verplanck's Point, reached the vicinity of New Windsor, on the west of the Hudson, where they were to erect log-huts for winter-quarters, on the 28th of October.  Dr. Thacher makes no mention of this Indian expedition, though he is careful to note all passing occurrences, and even the news from a distance.

[84] This winter expedition to the Indian country, is, in the MS. memoir, expanded into twenty-eight pages, which we will not materially abridge.

Soon after the army retired to winter quarters, and therefore in November, 1782, a large detachment was ordered to proceed to the head-waters of the Hudson, to repress the incursions which the Indians were making on the white settlements.  Our heroine, though not yet fully recoverd from her wound, volunteered to go.  They marched on the banks of the Hudson, and visited Fort Edward, Fort George, and Ticonderoga.  At Fort Edward they found Gen. Schuyler, on whom the compiler of the MS. memoir bestows two pages of panegyric.  Lake George, with the scenery around, also Ticonderoga and Crown Point, are described, occupying three or four pages.

From Ticonderoga the party struck off to the west.  The weather had hitherto been fine, though cold, with little or no snow on the ground.  But now they encountered a severe snowstorm, and marched through snow a foot deep; not "three feet deep," as says the *Female Review*.  Near the place now known as Johnsburgh, in Warren County, they had an encounter with a party of about a hundred Indians, who had just been murdering white families, and burning their houses.  These Indians fought desperately, but were overpowered, and put to flight.

"We came upon the Indians unexpectedly, at the distance of a pistolshot; and our first fire dealt terrible destruction among them.  Raising their horrid war-whoop, they returned our fire . . . . Three of our party were wounded, but not mortally.  Fifteen of the Indians were slain, and many more were wounded.  Numbers of the enemy eluded our shots, and made their escape into the woods.  Observing one man, light of foot, entering the forest, I happened to be foremost in pursuit of him.  I had scarcely come up with him, when he cried for quarter. My first impulse was to bayonet him; but an instant sympathy turned away the pointed steel. My next thought was, that his imperfect Indian dialect was counterfeit.  Thrusting my hand into his bosom, and making a wide rent in his inner garment, I discovered that he was the child of white parents, while his face, and his heart too, were as black as those of any savage.

270

through the wilderness.   She was in a party commanded by Capt.
Mills.   Not far from Bradport, an English settlement, the snow
having fallen three feet deep, they saw a man fleeing for his life.*
On inquiry, he informed, that the Indians had surrounded his
house, and were then in the heat of their butchery.   Hastening with
him to the place, they found the infernals had not finished their
hellish sacrifices.   The house was on fire, his wife mangled and lay
bleeding on the threshold.   Two children were hung by their heels;
one scalped, and yet alive; the other dead, with a tomahawk in its
brains.   They took them.   Females, have fortitude.   The daunt-

*The shades of evening were now settling down about us.   Returning with our captive
white Indian to the general slaughter-ground, a scene of indescribable horror presented itself
to our view.   The flames had levelled the house [of the man whom they saw fleeing for his life]
nearly to the earth.   The mother lay dead and horribly mangled a few feet from the threshold.
Two children were hung by their heels upon a tree," &c.   "While this was going on, a fine little
girl was discovered by her piteous plaints.   She had concealed herself under some straw.   She
was brought forth, not only stiff with the cold, but having a bad wound in the shoulder from a
tomahawk.   At sight of her, the wretched father sunk down upon the snow, as if never again
to rise, exhausted by the loss of blood from his own wound, as well as by the scene that surrounded him . . .

We now retraced our course to Fort Edward, frequently tinging the snow and ice with our
own blood.   Our shoes were worn through, and our clothing torn by the thick undergrowth of
the forest."

Here two pages are devoted to the tragic story of Jane McCrea, murdered by the Indians,
on the advance of Burgoyne's army, in August, 1777.   Six pages are then occupied with a brief
résumé of the Northern campaign of 1777, especially the battle of Bemis's Heights, on the 7th
of October; taken from Thacher's "Military Journal" and other histories.

At Albany, the MS. memoir affirms that she was sent for by Gen. Schuyler to visit him at
his residence, and complimented for her distinguished bravery in the Indian expedition.   Six
or seven pages are given to this interview, and to the conversation which is said to have there
taken place.   One of Gen. Schuyler's daughters, recently married to Col. Alex. Hamilton, is
introduced as detailing to our heroine the friendly reception given by the family to Gens.
Burgoyne, Philips, Reidesel, the Baroness Reidesel, Lady Acland, and their children, after the
surrender at Saratoga, including what was said and done on that occasion.   Credat Judaeus

"About the last of January, 1783, we reached the winter-cantonments of the army on the
Hudson, having seen hard service, but without having lost a man.   Scarcely had I taken a
night's repose in camp before the expressions hero, champion, victor, applied to myself, ran
currently through my regiment.   I have since thought it wonderful that I was not inflated
with pride, which sometimes lifts one above himself into the airy region of fools."   Not Deborah Sampson, but Mr. Mann, the compiler of the MS. memoir, is responsible for this language and the preceding statements.

less of your sex thrust her hand into the bosom of one, and rent his vesture.  The effect was the discovery of his being of the complexion of an Englishman, except where he was painted.  They sent him to Head Quarters, but executed the rest on the spot.

Before they reached the army, their feet once more crimsoned the snow—a token of their sufferings.  But her name resounded with plaudits; which would have been enhanced had the discovery of her sex then taken place.

## CHAPTER IX

She goes to live in a General Officer's family.  Miscellaneous incidents.  Marches with 1,500 men for the suppression of a mutiny among the American soldiers at Philadelphia.  Has a violent sickness and is carried to the hospital in this city.  Discovery of Sex.  A young Lady conceives an attachment for our blooming soldier.

IN the Spring of 1783, peace began to be the general topic; and which was actually announced to Congress.  A building was erected in which the officers held their concerts.  It would contain a brigade at a time for the exercise of public worship.  The timber was cut and drawn together by the soldiers, and mostly sawn by hand.  Our heroine worked against any hardy soldier, without any advantage in her yoke.  In its raising, a joist fell and carried her from a considerable height to the ground; but without doing any essential injury, except the dislocation of her nose and ancle.[85]

On the first of April, Gen. Paterson selected her for his Waiter; as he had previously become acquainted with her heroism and

85 There is no reference in the MS. memoir to anything of this sort.

fidelity.[86]   Cessation of hostilities was proclaimed on the 19th.[87] The honorary badge of distinction, as established by Gen. Washington, had been conferred on her; but for what particular exploit I cannot say.   Her business was here much less intense; and she found a superior school for improvement.

The General's attachment towards his new attendant was daily increasing.   Her martial deportment, blended with the milder graces and vivacity of her sex and youth, filled him with admiration and wonder.   Anxious to avail himself of every advantage to inspire his troops with emulation in the cause of their country, it is

86 "Directly after our return to headquarters, I found myself appointed waiter, or, as the more courtly phrase is, aide-de-camp, to my much-esteemed general, Paterson, and taken into his family.   This was in consequence of the illness of Major Haskell, who had served as his aide."

Dr. Thacher speaks of Major Haskell as being aide-de-camp to Gen. Paterson, and says he was a native of Rochester, Mass.   It is not very probable that Robert Shurtliffe should have been taken from the ranks, or from the position of sergeant, which she is said to have held, to be aide-de-camp to a general officer.

"Waiter" usually means a personal servant.—what in modern Army phrase is termed a "striker."—[ED.]

"I was furnished with a good horse and fine equipments, and found myself surrounded with the comforts, and even the elegancies, of life.   I no longer slept on a pallet of straw on the damp, cold ground, but on a good feather-bed.   And here, I presume, curiosity will be awake to inquire whether I always slept alone; and if not, with whom, and on what terms.   I will tell the truth frankly, and challenge contradiction.   In the first place, a soldier has not always his choice of lodgings or of bed-fellows.   He often lies down in promiscuous repose with his companions, without other partition than his blanket, his knapsack, and his musket.

"But, in Gen. Paterson's family, my couch invited to soft, undisturbed repose, such as I actually enjoyed.   My bed-companions were, sometimes one officer, and sometimes another. But no one was inferior to myself, either in rank or in virtuous principle, to say the least and the worst of them.   They as little suspected my sex, as I suspected them of a disposition to violate its chastity, had I been willing to expose myself to them and to act the wanton.   If this explanation is not satisfactory, if any still imagine that in my situation nothing short of a continned miracle could have kept me unpolluted, I must content myself with the inward satisfaction which conscious purity and virtue always afford, leaving them to struggle as they may with their doubts on the subject."

There is reason to believe that all the while she slept alone.

87 The Preliminary Treaty of Peace was signed at Paris, November 30, 1782, but not published by royal proclamation in London till February 15, 1783.   The cessation of hostilities was proclaimed in the American camp, by order of Gen. Washington, on the eighth anniversary of the battle of Lexington.

said, perhaps justly, that when he saw a delinquency or faint-
heartedness in his men, he often referred them to some heroic
achievement of his smock-faced boy, or convinced them by an ocular
example.[88]

Knowing she had his commendations, she found new stimula-
tions for perseverance, and scarcely any injunctions would have
been too severe for her compliance.   Hence it seems he was led to
conceive that such an assemblage of courage and refinement could
exist but in the superior order of his sex; and that such a youth was
highly calculated to shine either in the sphere of war, or in the
profession of a gentleman of taste and philosophic refinement.

Thus, Females, whilst you see the avidity of a maid in her
teens confronting dangers and made a veteran example in war, you
need only half the assiduity in your proper, domestic sphere, to
render your charms completely irresistible.

General orders were, every warm season, for the soldiers to go
into the water, as well to exercise themselves in the art of swimming,
as to clean their bodies.[89]   These injunctions were so directly in
point, that her compliance with them would unavoidably have been
unbosoming the delicate secret.   To have pled indisposition would
have been an argument against her; as the cold bath might have
wrought her cure: and to have intimated cowardice would have
entitled her to less lenity than when before in the Ferry.   So, after
lying awake the first night, she concluded to be the first to rise at
roll call.   Accordingly, the regiment paraded and marched to the
river.   She was expert in undressing with the rest.   After they
were mostly in the water, what should ravish her ear but the sound
of a sweet fountain, that percolated over a high rock near the
river's brink.   It was thickly enclosed with the aspen and alder.

88 Here belongs the story related in the Appendix, respecting her journey from West
Point to "a place called the Clove."

89 This account is omitted in the MS. memoir   It is wholly improbable.

Thither she unnoticed retired. And whilst the Hudson swelled with the multitude of masculine bodies, a beautiful rivulet answered every purpose of bathing a more delicate form. Nor were there any old, letcherous, sanctified Elders to peep through the rustling leaves to be inflamed with her charms.

One more incident may amuse those ladies, who are fond of angling.[90]—One day, she, with some others, at the ebb of tide, went to the Hudson for this purpose. Near the boat, she discovered a beautiful azure rock, well situated for fishing. Too careless of her famed predecessor's disposition, she disembarked from the boat to the rock. Soon after, they purposely weighed anchor and left her surrounded with water. She continued not long before, to her surprise, as well as the rest, the rock became a self-moving vehicle, and sat out to overtake her company. Dreading the passage, she leaped into the water and mire and had many severe struggles before she reached land. The rock proved a prodigious Tortoise. And lest antiquity should not be cured of credulity and superstition, [and] thereby enhance the prodigy to their generation—that a female was once a navigator on the back of a Tortoise, that he finally swallowed her and some time after spouted her alive on the fertile land;—it is only needful to mention that they gaffed him, with much difficulty towed him reluctant to the shore, and soon after, on a day of festival, ate him.

This Summer a detachment of 1,500 men was ordered to march to Philadelphia for the suppression of a mutiny among the American soldiers.[91] She did not go till four days after the General

90 This unlikely story is also omitted in the MS. memoir.

91 At the close of the war, it was found extremely difficult, and indeed impossible, to pay off the soldiers of the Continental army. The United States were a nation; but there was no national government,—only a confederation. Congress did not possess the power of taxation; and no means existed for raising a revenue for national purposes. The powers of government, so far as any existed, were held by the several States, which were slow to exercise them when they were likely to bear hard upon the people. Congress had resorted to loans; immense quantities of paper-money had been issued during the war, but the Continental currency had depreciated rapidly, till in the latter part of 1780, it became worthless, and ceased to circulate.

left West Point.   She then rode in company with four gentlemen,
and had a richly variegated prospect through the Jersies and a part
of Pennsylvania.   In Goshen they were invited to a ball; where she
was pleased to see, especially in the ladies, the brilliancy and polite-
ness of those in New England.   They were here detained two days
on account of Lieut. Stone, who was confined for a duel with Capt.
Hitchcock, who was killed.[92]   She found the troops encamped on a
hill; from which, they had a fine prospect of the city and of the
Allegany, which rises majestic over the intervening country.   Here
she had frequent occasion to visit the city, sometimes on business,
and often curiosity led her to view its magnificence.   The gentility
of her dress and agreeable mien gained her access to company of
both sexes of rank and elegance.

The storm of war having subsided, an agreeable prospect once
more gleamed on the face of Columbia.   But fortune had more dan-

There were therefore no funds, at the close of the war, to pay the troops.  The greater part
of them bore the evil with commendable patience, submitting to it as a matter of unavoidable
necessity.   In many cases, however, there was discontent, and, in a few cases, as here, open
mutiny.

A small body of Pennsylvania troops—Thacher says about eighty—encamped at Lan-
caster, in that State, in the month of June, 1783, clamored for their pay, rose in revolt, and
marched to Philadelphia, sixty-seven miles distant, determined to enforce their claim upon Congress at the point of the bayonet.   Arriving in that city on the 29th of that month, they proceeded to the barracks; and being joined by two hundred troops from Carolina, and obtaining
artillery, they marched, with drums beating, to the State House, where Congress was then
assembled.   Placing guards at every door, they sent in a message, accompanied with a threat,
that, if their demands were not complied with in twenty minutes, they would proceed to open
violence.

The members of Congress succeeded, however, in making their escape, and sent information of the affair to Gen. Washington, who immediately ordered a detachment of troops on
whom he could rely, fifteen hundred strong, under the command of Major-Gen. Robert Howe,
to proceed to Philadelphia, and to  uppress the mutiny.   This affair gave occasion for our
heroine to visit Philadelphia.   Happily, the insurgents submitted at once.   Some of the ring-
leaders were tried and sentenced, two to suffer death, and four to other punishment.   But Cou-
gress pardoned them all.   Dr. Thacher notices this affair.   He says, "On the 29th of June, about
eighty new-levy soldiers of the Pennsylvania line marched to Philadelphia," &c.

92  The duel took place at Goshen.   Very likely, it originated in that ballroom.   "We
left Hitchcock, who had been a good officer, dead upon the field, and Stone in prison.   This detained us two days."

gers and toils assigned her. An epidemic disorder raged in the city: and she was quickly selected a victim, and carried once more to the hospital with all the horrible apprehensions of her situation.[93] Death itself could scarcely have presented a more gloomy prospect: and that seemed not far distant, as multitudes were daily carried to the Potter's Field. She begged not to be left in the loathsome bunks of soldiers. Accordingly, she was lodged in a third loft, where were two other officers of the same line, who soon died. Alone she was then left to condole her wretchedness: except Doctor Bana[94] and the Matron, Mrs. Parker, whose solicitude she remembers with gratitude.

How poignantly must reflection have here brought to her memory those soft and tranquil seasons, wherein she so often deprived herself the midsummer's morning dream, to breathe with the lark the fresh incense of morning!—when with hasty steps she brushed the dews from vegetation, to meet the sun on the rising grounds*: by which, to catch fresh hints of Creation, and to inhale Thee, buxom health, from every opening flower! But she is now, not indeed, like Egyptian mummies, wrapped in fine linen and laid on beds of spices, but on the naked floor, anticipating the Archer Death, in all the frightful forms of his equipage.

But at length she was deprived of the faculty of reflection. The Archer was about to execute his last office. The inhuman sextons had drawn their allowance, and upon her vesture they were casting lots. One Jones, the only English nurse, at that instant

93 "A malignant fever was then raging in Philadelphia, particularly among the troops stationed there and in the vicinity. I was soon seized with it. I scarcely felt its symptoms before I was carried to the hospital. All I distinctly remember was the prospect of death, which seemed not far distant. I was thrown into a loathsome bunk, out of which had just been removed a corpse for burial; soon after which, I became utterly insensible."—[MS. Memoir.]

Would the authorities of the hospital have treated in this manner an aide-de-camp of Gen. Paterson?

94 Dr. Binney, the surgeon of the hospital, is here intended. Dr. Thacher mentions that he dined in Philadelphia, September 9, 1782, with "Doctor Binney of the hospital."

*Mr. Mann had read Gray's *Elegy!*

coming in, she once more rallied the small remains of nature and gave signs of life. The sextons withdrew, and Jones informed the Matron such a one was yet alive; which she discredited.[95] Doctor Bana at that instant entered; and putting his hand in her bosom to feel her pulse, was surprised to find an inner waist-coat lightly compressing her breasts. Ripping it in haste, he was still more shocked, not only on finding life, but the breasts and other tokens of a female.[96] Immediately she was removed into the Matron's own apartment; and from that time to her recovery, treated with all the care that art and expense could bestow.[97]

95 "It was not long before I came to some degree of consciousness, when I perceived preparations making for my burial. I heard the funeral-undertakers quarrelling about some part of my clothing, which each of them wished to possess. One Jones, the only English-speaking nurse in the hospital, coming in, I succeeded, by an almost superhuman effort, in convincing him that I was still alive. I well remember that he not only threatened these monsters, but used actual force to prevent their dragging me to the Potter's Field, the place of burial for strangers. The undertakers at length withdrew, when Jones informed the worthy matron, Mrs. Parker, that Robert Shurtliffe, a soldier in bunk No.—, who had been supposed to be dead, was actually alive. This she was inclined to doubt. It was said that they came to ascertain the fact. But I know it not; for I had sunk once more into a state resembling death." —[MS. Memoir.]

96 "They had scarcely retired a second time, when Dr. Binney, the surgeon, visited the hospital, to whom Jones made known the fact of my partial re-animation. He immediately came to my apartment, and called me by name. Though I distinctly heard him, I could make no reply. He turned away for a moment to some other patients. I thought he had left me again to the ravenous undertakers. By a great effort, I made a kind of gurgling in my throat to call his attention to me. Never can I forget his elastic step, and apparently deep emotion, as he sprang to my bed-side. Thrusting his hand into my bosom to ascertain if there were motion at the heart, he was surprised at finding an inner vest lightly compressing my breasts, the instant removal of which not only ascertained the fact of life, but disclosed the fact that I was a woman! He forced, by some instrument, a medicine into my stomach, which greatly revived me, and caused me to exhibit further signs of life."—[ibid.]

97 This remarkable discovery the benevolent surgeon imparted to none but Mrs. Parker, the matron of the hospital, charging her to confine the knowledge of it to her own bosom. Our heroine was, after being conveyed to Mrs. Parker's apartment, nursed with the greatest care. She now slowly recovered; and, as soon as she was able to ride, she was taken to Dr. Binney's house, and treated with the most delicate attention. As her recovery proceeded, she began to suspect that a discovery had been made, to her most unwelcome. She could account in no other way for the tenderness with which she was treated. Her kind friends, Mrs. Parker and Dr. Binney, were careful to conceal from her the knowledge they had acquired; but it was evident to her mind that they did not expect that she would resume her military attire.

"But in this," says Deborah, "they were mistaken; and so was I mistaken in the use which

The amiable physician had the prudence to conceal this important discovery from every breast but the Matron. From that time, the once more discovered female became a welcome guest in their families. And they recommended her to others, as an object worthy their attention and affection. But there remains another event, perhaps, the most unparalleled of its kind, to be unfolded.

A young lady of the suburbs of Baltimore, beautiful in form, blest with a well cultivated mind, and a fortune, had often conversed with this illustrious soldier.[98] The gracefulness of her mien, mixed with her dignified, martial airs, enraptured her. At first she attempted to check the impulse, as the effect of a giddy passion; but at length suffered it to play about her heart unchided. Cupid, impatient, at length urged his quiver too far, and wounded the seat of love. O Love! how powerful is your influence! how unlimited your domain! The gallant Solomon could not have composed three thousand proverbs and his madrigals to his love, without much of your conviviality. The illuminations of Venus were known in those days. And it was by her rays the Preacher of love so often strolled with his Egyptian belles in his vineyard, when the flowers appeared on the earth, the mandrakes gave a good smell, and the time of the singing of birds had come; when they reciprocated their love amidst the dews of dawn.

I presumed would be made of the discovery of my sex. Emaciated and pallid, I was introduced by the good Dr. Binney to his wife and daughters as a young and gallant soldier who had met in battle the enemies of our country, and had now risen, as it were, from the bed of death. This introduction was sufficient to commend me to their warmest sympathies. In their company, I rambled through the streets of the city, attended public exhibitions, sailed upon the Delaware, and strolled in the groves and flowery meads. The Doctor had no fears of the result. I was admitted as a guest in many wealthy families, still known only as a Continental soldier."—[*Ib.*]

98 This love-story is told in the MS. memoir with considerable variation. It is there said that the young lady, the writer of the ensuing letter, was seventeen years of age, the daughter of wealthy parents in Baltimore, and now an orphan; that the acquaintance commenced in September, 1781, during the stay of the American army at Annapolis when on its way to Yorktown, and that they became mutually and tenderly attached. The letter in the MS. memoir is better written.

Sufficient it is that this love is preserved, and that it will remain incontrovertible. And happy it is, that it is not only enjoyed by the prince of the inner pavillion. It leaps upon the mountains; and, under the shadow of the apple tree, it is sweet to the taste. From the moss covered cottage it is pursued, even amidst the thunders of war and the distraction of elements. And the nymph of Maryland was as much entitled to it, as the mistress of him who had the caressing of a thousand. Hers was sentimental and established: and she was miserable from the thought that it might not be interchangeable.

On this account, the productions of her plantation were no longer relished with pleasure. The music of her groves became dissonant, her grottos too solitary, and the rivulets purled but for her discontent. From these she flew in search of him whom her soul loved, among the bustling roar of the city. And the third morning after she was confined in the hospital, a courier delivered her a letter and a handkerchief full of choice fruit. Inclosed was the substance of the following:

Dear Sir,

Fraught with the feelings of a friend, who is, doubtless, beyond your conception, interested in your health and happiness, I take liberty to address you with a frankness, which nothing but the purest friendship and affection can palliate. Know, then, that the charms I first read in your visage brought a passion into my bosom for which I could not account. If it was from the thing called Love, I was before mostly ignorant of it, and strove to stifle the fugitive; though I confess the indulgence was agreeable. But repeated interviews with you kindled it into a flame, I do not now blush to own: and should it meet a generous return, I shall not reproach myself for its indulgence. I have long sought to hear of your apartment: And how painful is the news I this moment receive, that you are sick, if alive, in the hospital! Your complicated nerves will not admit of writing. But inform the bearer, if you are necessitated for any thing, that can conduce to your comfort. If you recover, and think proper to enquire my name, I will give you an opportunity. But if death is to terminate your existence there, let your last senses be impressed with the reflection, that you die not without one more friend, whose tears will bedew your funeral obsequies. Adieu.

Some have been charmed, others surprised by love in the dark, and from an unexpected quarter; but she alone can conceive what effect, what perturbation, such a declaration had on her mind; whose nearest prospect seemed that of her own dissolution. She humbly returned her gratitude, but happily was not in want of money, owing to a prize she in company had found in the British lines, consisting of clothes, plate and coin.[99] In the evening she received a billet inclosing two guineas. The like favors were continued during her illness.[100] But she knew not in whose bosom the passion vibrated. Her recovery must make the next chapter eventful.

## CHAPTER X

Her critical situation. Commences a tour towards the Ohio with some gentlemen. Interview with her lover. They meet a terrible tempest. She is left sick with the Indians.

HEALTH having reanimated the so much admired Virago, one might conclude she had business enough on hand: And, gracious Powers! what had she not on her heart and mind? Suspicious that a discovery had been made during her illness, every zephyr became an ill-fated omen and every salutation, a mandate to summon her to a retribution for her imposition on the maculine character.

Such embarrassments foreboded the winding up of her drama. And she was doubtless careful to picture the event in the blackest colours. A retrospection of her life must have brought, to her mind a contrast, unknown to many and dreaded by all. But having stood at helm during the severity of the storm, she concluded, if a concession must be extorted from her, it might appear less dastardly after a beautiful, serene day had commenced; and that it mattered little whether it should happen among the insatiable throng of the city, or the ruder few of the desolate heath. Thus the lioness, having pervaded every toil and danger from the hounds and hunters, at length, cornered on all sides, disdaining their fury, yields herself a prey.

99, 100 No statements like these appear in the MS. memoir.

Doctor Bana was now waiting a convenient opportunity to divulge to her his suspicion of her sex. He often found her dejected; and as he guessed the cause introduced lively discourse. She had the happiness to recommend herself much to the esteem of his discreet and amiable daughter. And the Doctor was fond that so promising a stripling should often gallant them into the city and country villages. The unruffled surface of a summer's sea was also often a witness to their pastimes.[101] This rare species of innocent recreation was doubtless peculiarly gratifying to the Doctor; as his mind could not be more at rest on his daughters' account. Nor need they think themselves chagrined, when it is known they once had a female gallant; on the strength of whose arm and sword they would have depended in case of danger.

After she had resumed her regimentals to rejoin the troops, the Doctor, availing himself of a private conference, asked her, whether she had any particular confidant in the army? She said, no; and trembling, would have disclosed the secret: but he, seeing her confusion, waived the discourse. To divert her mind he proposed her taking a tour towards the Ohio with Col. Tupper[102] of

101 By "a summer's sea," here, is meant the River Delaware, on which they sometimes enjoyed a sail. (See note 97.) Mrs. Ellet here introduces a love adventure between Deborah and a niece of the doctor, which corresponds with that between the former and the Baltimore lady.

102 Col. (afterwards Gen.) Benjamin Tupper was born in Sharon, then a part of Stoughton, Mass., in 1738. He was a private soldier in the "Old French War," from 1755 to 1762. He was in the military service of his country during the whole Revolutionary War; first as major, then as colonel, of the Eleventh Massachusetts Regiment. Very soon after the war, he, with Gen. Rufus Putnam and other officers of the Continental army, united in a plan for the settlement of what is now the State of Ohio. The journey mentioned in the text may have been connected with this design. In the summer of 1785, Gen. Tupper went as far as Pittsburgh, with the intention of making a survey of a portion of the lands in that State, but was prevented by the unfriendly spirit of the Indian tribes at that time. A survey of seven ranges of townships in Ohio was completed in the summer of 1786, under his direction. With two wagons, one for his family, the other for their baggage, he went all the way from Chesterfield, Mass., then his home, to Marietta, Ohio, and, with others, commenced the settlement of that town in August, 1788. He died in June, 1792.—[S. P. Hildreth's *Early Settlers of Ohio.*]

It is not at all likely that Deborah Sampson accompanied Col. Tupper on such an expedition.

Massachusetts, Messrs. Forkson and Graham of Philadelphia; who were going, partly to contemplate the country and partly to discover minerals. Knowing the mineral rods were peculiar to her, he said, whilst the tour might be profitable it might be a restorative to her health, and an amusement to her mind.

Surprised to find this met her concurrence, he used some arguments to dissuade her from it: but finding her unequivocal, he enjoined it upon her to visit his house at her return; which she promised. And about the last of August, they set out from the *Conastoga Waggon* and went in the stage the first day to Baltimore which is eighty miles.

Next day, as she was viewing the town, she received a billet requesting her company at such a place. Though confident she had before seen the handwriting, she could not conjecture what was commencing. Prompted by curiosity she went; and being conducted into an elegant room, was struck with admiration, on finding alone, the amiable and all accomplished Miss————— of about seventeen, whom she had long thought a conspicuous ornament to her sex. The lady expressed surprise on seeing him, who, according to report, had died soon after she left the metropolis. An acquaintance being before established, mutual compliments passed between the lovers. The young lady confessed herself author of the anonymous letter.[103] And though uncertain of a concession—timorous as a young roe, yet pliant as the bending ozier, with the queen of love resident in her eyes, she rehearsed her plaint of love with that unreservedness which evinced the sincerity of her passion and exaltedness of soul. The soul is the emporium of love. Their blushes and palpitations were doubtless reciprocal; but, I judge, of a different nature. But while this liberal concession was the strongest evidence that she possessed love without desire of prostitution, and friendship without dissimulation; let it be remembered, to her honor, that her effusions flowed with that affability, prudence and dignified grace,

103 For the letter, see page 138.

which must have fired the breast of an anchorite—inanimate nature itself must have waked into life, and even the superstitious, cowled friar must have revoked his eternal vows of celibacy, and have flown to the embraces of an object exhibiting so many charms in her eloquence of love.

Thus, ye delicate, who would be candidates for the fruition of this noble, this angelic passion, it is refinement only that renders your beauty amiable, and even unreservedness, in either sex, agreeable.   The reverse is only a happy circumstance between vice and virtue.   While it there happily preys on every delicate sensation it renders the idea of enjoyment loathsome, and even hurries delicacy herself into distress.

Had this unfortunate lover uttered herself in an uncouth, illiterate, unpolished manner, every word would have lost its energy and all her charms become vapid on the senses.   Or, had she assumed the attire, the cunning of an harlot—the desperate simplicity of a young wanton; had she begun her subtle eloquence with a kiss; and with the poison of asps under her tongue, have represented her bed of embroidery filled with perfume, and finally have urged that the absence of the good man gave them an opportunity to riot in the extatic delights of love—while our young fugitive would have needed supernatural means to have answered the demands of venerious appetition, the simple might have found satiety in her seraglio: but Virtue would have continued on her throne in sullen sadness.   But this was not the case.   Though suspended between natural and artificial confusion—though sickness had abated her acuteness for the soft romances of love; she doubtless embraced the celestial maid, and wishing herself mistress of her superior charms, could not but participate in the genial warmth of a passion so irresistibly managed.   Knowledge intermixed with beauty and refinement, enkindles a warmth of the purest love; and, like the centre of the earth, commands the power of attraction.

284

She tarried in this school of animal philosophy the most of two. days; then promising to visit her in her return, proceeded on her journey.[104]

From Baltimore, passing Elk Ridge, they came to Alexandria in Virginia. Nine miles below is Mount Vernon, the seat of the illustrious Washington, which they visited. It is situated near a bend in the Potomak; where it is two miles wide. The area of the mount is 200 feet above the surface of the river. On either wing is a thick grove of flowering trees. Parallel with them are two spacious gardens, adorned with serpentine gravel walks, planted with weeping willows and shady shrubs. The mansion house is venerable and convenient. A lofty dome, 96 feet in length, supported by eight pillars, has a pleasing effect when viewed from thee water. This, with the assemblage of the green house, offices and servants' halls, bears the resemblance of a rural village; especially as the grass plats are interspersed with little copses, circular clumps and single trees. A small park on the margin of the river, where the English fallow deer and the American wild deer are alternately seen through the thickets by passengers on the river, adds a romantic and picturesque prospect to the whole scenery. Such are the philosophic shades to which the late Commander of the American Armies, and President of the nation, has now retired from a tumultuous and busy world.

104 Instead of this rhapsody, take the following, from the MS. memoir: "She received me with a dignified and yet familiar air. She apologized with infinite grace for overstepping the acknowledged bounds of female delicacy in making such an overture to a gentleman. She expressed great pleasure and much surprise at seeing me alive; having been led to suppose, from an account that reached her not long before, that I had died in the hospital. She confessed the tender sentiments of her heart, which had led her to seek this interview . . . . What could I do, what could I say, in such an exigency? How should I feel, on receiving such a declaration from such a heart? I could not act the hypocrite with such an artless girl; nor could I refuse the affection so warmly proffered, and so delicately expressed. But I could not then disclose to her the secret I was so anxious to conceal from all the world beside. In this state of embarrassment I continued the most of two days, and finally compromised the matter by promising to call on her again on my return from the West."

Their next route was to the southwestern parts of Virginia.* Having travelled some days, they came to a large river; when the gentlemen and guide disputed, whether it was the Monongahela, Yohogany, or the Ohio itself.¹⁰⁵ They concluded to wait till the fog, which was very thick, should be gone, that they might determine with more precision. But instead of dissipating it increased, and they heard thunder roll at a distance. On a sudden a most violent tempest of wind and rain commenced, accompanied with such perpetual lightning and peals of thunder, that all nature seemed in one combustible convulsion. The leeward side of a shelving rock illy screened them from the storm, which continued to rage the most of the night. Happily they were preserved, though one of their dogs became a victim to the electric fire. It is said he was so near their female companion when killed, that she could have reached him with a common staff.

Next day the weather was calm. They discharged their pieces in order to clean them; the report of which brought to their view six of the natives in warlike array. Many ceremonies were effected before they could be convinced of friendship. When effected, they solicited the guide to follow them; indicating by their rude noises and actions, they were much troubled. He refusing, their Adventuress laughed at his caution.¹⁰⁶ One of the Indians, observing this, ran to her, fired his arrow over her head, took a wreath of wampum, twined it about her waist, and bade her follow. She obeyed; though they checked her presumption. They conducted her to a cave; which she thinks is as great a natural curiosity as that of Madison's. They complimented her to enter

*I know not whether it was in this tour, that she visited the famous Cascade in Virginia, Madison's Cave on the North side of the Blue Ridge, and the passage of the Potomak through the same; which is one of the most august scenes in nature.

105 This river proved to be the Shenandoah.

106 "Observing that he [the guide] hesitated, I stepped forward with my gun, and offered to go in his place, at the same time laughing at his extreme caution. My companions taxed me with presumption and folly, but I was determined, then and always, not to be a coward."

nearly to the centre, fell on their faces; and whilst the cave echoed with their frightful yells and actions, our Adventuress, as usual first; which she durst not refuse. They followed; and advancing doubtless, thought of home. When they rose they ran to the further part, dragged three dead Indians out of the cave and laid their faces to the ground. Then climbing a rock, they rolled down immense stones; then whooping, first pointing to the sky, then to the stones, and then to the Indians, who were killed by the lightning the preceding day. Having convinced them, she understood it, and that the mate to a dog with her had shared the same fate, they conducted her to her company. They told her they had despaired of ever seeing her again; concluding her scalp was taken off when they heard the shouting. She jocosely extolled them for their champion courage, but not for their lenity; as they did not go to her relief. They all then went to the cave and attended their savage, funeral ceremonies.

The Indians went with them up the river, which they con cluded to be one of the Kanhawas. But in this they were mistaken; they being too much to the South. They hired one of the tribe to pilot them [107] over the Allegany. Passing the Jumetta Creek and the Fork of the Pennsylvania and Glade Roads, about 40 miles from the Jumetta, they came to the foot of the Dry Ridge.[108] Here they found trees whose fruit resembled the nectarine; and like it, delicious to the taste. Eating freely of it till observing the Indian did not, they desisted. And happily so; for it came near proving mortal. Its first effect was sickness at the stomach. The descendant of her who is accused of having been too heedless of the bewitching charm of curiosity, puked and bled at the nose, till she was unable to walk. The Indian was missing; but soon

107 "Two of the Indians we hired as guides over the next range of the Alleghanies, which is more lofty and majestic than the Blue Ridge, the range we had already passed. There are two Kenhawas."

108 The Laurel Mountains, the western range of the Alleghanies.

came with a handful of roots, which, being bruised and applied to her nose and each side of her neck, stopped the blood and sickness.

Hence they visited a tribe near a place, called Medskar. She was here so indisposed she could not proceed on the journey. Her illness proved a relapse of her fever.[109]  The pilot interceded with the King for her to tarry with them till the return of her company; which he said would be at the close of one moon. Being convinced they were no spies, nor invaders, he consented. He then ordered an Indian and his squaw to doctor her; telling them, the boy would eat good, when fattened.[110]—She remarks that their medicines always had a more sensible effect, than those of common physicians. Thus in a short time she recovered. But I shall not attempt to recount all her sufferings, especially by hunger, but a more intense torture of mind, during this barbarous servitude.

Her aim was, never to discover the least cowardice, but always to laugh at their threats. A striking instance of this she exemplified at their coronation of a new King. Her master, like a hell-hound, hooting her into the square, where were many kettles of water boiling, told her, he was going to have a slice of her for dinner. Being the only white man (a girl!) among them, she was instantly surrounded by the infernals. She asked him if he ever ate Englishmen? He answered, *good omskuock!* She then told him he must keep her better, or she should never do to eat. Some understood her; and giving a terrible shout, first told her to cut a notch in the stone kalendar, then putting her hands on the king's head, she joined the dance and fared with the rest. Ladies at a civilized ball may be insensible of this scene.

The reader keeps in view, I suppose, that all female courage is not jeoparded in this manner. I am perfectly enraptured with those females who exhibit the most refined sensibility and skill in

109  It was a return of the fever she had in Philadelphia.

110  This was said to try her courage.

their sweet domestic round, and who can show a group of well-bred boys and girls. But I must aver I am also happy, if this rare female has filled that vacuity, more or less in every one's bosom, by the execution of the worst propensities, for, by similitude, we may anticipate that one-half of the world in future are to have less goads in their consciences, and the other, faster accumulating a fund of more useful acquisition.

## CHAPTER XI

A hunting tour. She kills her Indian companion. Comes near perishing in the wilderness. Liberates an English Girl, condemned to be burnt. Their return to Philadelphia.

AURORA had scarcely purpled the East after the coronation, before a large company, including our Adventuress, sat out for hunting.[111] She quickly espied a wild turkey on a high tree, which she killed. Then, with actions peculiar to Indians, they surrounded her to extol her being quick-sighted and a good marksman. They encamped that night under an hickory; through which was a chasm cut sufficient for two to walk abreast. In the morning they divided into parties. An old Indian, a boy and our Adventuress composed one. Elate with the beauty of the morning, the old Indian led off about the sun's rising. Ascending a large hill, the dogs started a buffalo, which she shot before the Indian got sight. The boy was much elevated with her alertness: but the Indian discovered much envy. He however craved the butchering; which she granted, reserving the skin to herself. Making a hearty meal of the buffalo, they travelled all day, without killing any more game, except three turkeys.

Night having again drawn her sable curtains, they took lodgings under a large sycamore: but she had an unusual aversion to

111 "Aurora now, fair daughter of the dawn,
Sprinkled with rosy light the dewy lawn."—[*Pope's Iliad.*]

sleep as she mistrusted the same of the Indian.  At length she became satisfied he had a fatal design on her life.  Feigning herself asleep, she waited till he had crawled within musket reach of her; when to her surprise she discovered a hatchet in his hand. Without hesitating, she leaped upon her feet, and shot him through the breast, before he had time to beg quarter.

The explosion of the gun awaked the boy, who, seeing his countryman dead, rent his clothes, whooped and tore the ground like a mad bull; fearing he should share the same fate.  She pacified him by observing it was in defence of her own life she had killed him; and that, if he would conduct well, and promise on his life to conceal it from his countrymen, he should fare well.  He swore allegiance.  And in the morning, they hoisted an old log and left the barbarian under it.

Behold now a young female, who might doubtless have shone conspicuous with others of her sex in their domestic sphere, reduced to the forlorn necessity of roaming in a desolate wilderness; whose only companion, except wild beasts, is an Indian boy; whose only sustenance such as an uncultivated glebe affords; and whose awful prospect, that of perishing at so great a distance from all succors of humanity!  To those who maintain the doctrines of fatalism, she is certainly a subject of their greatest sympathy.  And even to those who may be unwilling to adduce any other traits in her life but wild, dissolute freaks of fancy, to be gratified at her option, she is rather an object of pity than contempt.

At night, almost spent with hunger and fatigue, they lay down to repose.  But they were immediately alarmed by voracious beasts of prey.  Their only safety, and that not sure, was to lodge themselves in a high tree.  The fires they had kindled gained their approach and encreased their howlings.  The boy was so frightened he ran up the tree like a squirrel.  She followed, assisted doubtless by the same thing.  Though drowsy they durst not sleep, lest

290

they should fall. With the strap of her fusee and handkerchief, she made herself fast to a limb and slept till day. It rained by showers the most of the night. After she awoke her second thought was of the boy. She spoke to him; but he did not answer. Looking up at him, she was surprised to see him intently employed in disengaging his hair, which he had faithfully twined round the branches.

After descending the tree and threshing themselves till they could walk, they shaped their course for the East; but God only knows which way they went. Towards night they discovered a huge precipice, but found it inaccessible till they had travelled nearly four miles round it. Then ascending, they came to a rivulet of good water, and by it took their abode during the night. In the morning they were at a stand, whether to descend, or attempt to reach its summit. The poor boy wept bitterly; which she says were the first tears she ever saw an Indian shed. They concluded on the latter, as their ascent might possibly discover some prospect of escape. Passing many sharp ledges, they came to a spot of bear's grass, on which she reclined, thinking the period of her life was hastening with great rapidity, The following may not be a rude sketch of her reflections on this occasion:

"Where am I! What have I been doing! Why did I leave my native land, to grieve the breast of a parent who had doubtless shed floods of tears in my absence, and whose cup of calamities seemed before but too full! But here I am, where I think, human feet never before trod. And though I have relatives, and perhaps, friends, they can obtain no knowledge of me, not even to close my eyes when death shall have done its office, nor to perform the last sad demand of nature, which is to consign the body to the dust!— But stop! vain imagination! There is a Deity, from whom I cannot be hidden. It is He who shapes my end. My soul what thinkest thou of immortality, of the world, into which thou art so rapidly hastening! No words, no sagacity can disclose my apprehensions.

Every doubt wears the aspect of horror, and would certainly overwhelm me, were it not for a few gleams of hope which dart across the tremendous gloom.  Happy methinks I should be, could I but utter even to myself the anguish of my mind, thus suspended·between the extremes of infinite joy, or eternal misery!  It appears I have but just now emerged from sleep!  Oh, how have I employed my time!  In what delirium has the thread of my life thus far been spun!  While the planets in their courses, the sun and stars in their spheres have lent their refulgent beams—perhaps I have been lighted only to perdition!"

While in this extacy she availed herself of the opportunity to write to her female companion; and in it inclosed a letter to her mother, in hopes it might, by means of the boy, reach her.

Dear Miss———,
     Perhaps you are the nearest friend I have.  But a few hours must inevitably waft me to an infinite distance from all sublunary enjoyments, and fix me in a state of changeless retribution.  Three years having made me the sport of fortune I am at length doomed to end my existence in a dreary wilderness, unattended, except by an Indian boy.  If you receive these lines, remember they come from one, who sincerely loves you.  But my amiable friend, forgive my imperfections, and forget you ever had affection for one so unworthy the name of

YOUR OWN SEX.

While in this position she heard the report of a gun.  Starting about, she missed the boy and her fusee.  She could not recollect whether he was with her when she sat down, or not.  But summoning all her strength and resolution, she had nearly reached the summit of the mountain, when she met the boy.  He told her he fired that she might come to him; but as she did not, he concluded she would do to eat, and was going to fill his belly with good *omskuock*.[112]  He seemed glad he had found something to relieve them.  Giving her a scrohon and four grapes, he bid her follow him.  Coming to an immense rock, he crept through a fissure; and with much

112 It is otherwise in the MS. memoir.  "He said he discharged the gun, that I might come to him; but, as I did not, he concluded that I was dead.  Soon after, we found some ground-nuts," &c.  These adventures in the wilderness are related with greater fulness, and in far better language.

ado, she after him.   Here they found wild scrohons, hops, gourds, ground-nuts and beans.   Though mostly rotten, they ate some of them, and were revived.   Then, at a great distance, opening to their view a large river or lake and vastly high mountains.   Whilst they were contriving how to get to the river, they heard the firing of small arms, which they answered and had returns.

Descending the precipice, they came to large rocks of isinglass* and brooks of choice water.   At its base they came up with a large company of Indians, who had been to Detroit to draw blankets and military stores.   But to her surprise, who should make one of the company, but a dejected young female!   At once she was anxious to learn her history; which she soon did at private interviews.   She said she was taken from Cherry Valley—had been sold many times, but expected to be sold no more!—Tears prevented her proceeding.

In three days they arrived at the place from whence she first sat out on hunting.   The old chief accused her for having run away after the Englishmen: and it was the boy, with the interposition of Providence, saved her life.   She here quickly learned that her unfortunate sister sufferer was to be *burnt,* after they should have one court and a pawaw, for letting fall a papoos,† when travelling with an intense load.   At once she resolved to liberate her if any thing short of her own life would do it.   Her plan was thus concerted: she requested to marry one of their girls.   They haughtily refused; but concluded, for so much, she might have the white girl.   Begging her reprieve till the return of her company, which happened the next day, they all liberally contributed, and thus paid her ransom. The poor girl fainted at the news.   But hearing the conditions, she seemed suspended in choice, whether to suffer an ignominious death, or be bought as a booty to be ravished of her virgin purity:[113]—for she

*Mica.
†Indian baby.

113 She regarded any marriage which could take place under existing circumstances as of no validity.   The Indians had no marriage ceremonies.

intimated that, among all the cruelties of these savages, they had
never intruded on her chastity.   Her intended husband privately
told her, the rites of the marriage bed should be deferred till the
ceremony should be solemnized in the land of civilization.   At
night a bear's skin was spread for their lodging; but like a timorous
bride, sleep was to her a stranger.   On their return to Philadelphia
they purchased her a suit of clothes; but she, unable to express her
gratitude, received them on her knees, and was doubtless glad to
relinquish her sham marriage, and to be sent to her uncle; who she
said, lived in James City.[114]

Arrived at Baltimore, she repaired to visit her companion, who
became much affected with her history.   She now thought it time
to divert herself of the mask; at least to divert a passion, which she
feared had too much involved one of the choicest of her sex.   After
thanking her for her generous esteem, and many evasive apologies—
that she was but a stripling soldier, and that had she inclinations,
indigence would forbid her settling in the world: The beautiful
nymph replied that, sooner than a concession should take place
with the least reluctance, she would forfeit every enjoyment of
connubial bliss: but, she added, if want of interest was the only
obstacle, she was quickly to come into the possession of an ample
fortune; and finally intimated her desire, that she should not leave
her.[115]

114 "The next day, my company [Col. Tupper and the other gentlemen] fortunately
reached the Indian camp, on their return home.   The stipulated ransom being paid between
us, we took the liberated girl to Baltimore in our party.   There we procured for her a liberal
subscription in apparel and money.   Hence we sent her, with a heart overflowing with gratitude, to her parents, who, we were by accident informed, had removed, just after the surrender
of Cornwallis, to Williamsburg, in Virginia."   If this unfortunate maid was taken, as is said
above, from Cherry Valley, she must have been of New England origin, and her parents would
not at this time reside on the James River in Virginia.   This story of the captive girl must therefore be received with some distrust.

115 "No sooner had I returned to Baltimore than an irresistible attraction drew me again
into the presence of the amiable Miss P.——.   I went with the full determination to confess
to her who and what I was.   How should I do this?   I resolved to prepare the way for such a
disclosure by endeavoring to weaken, without wounding, the passion in her breast.   I told

Touched with such a pathetic assemblage of love and beauty, she burst into tears, and told her she would go to the northward, settle her affairs, and in the ensuing spring, if health should permit, would return; when, if her person could conduce to her happiness, she should be richly entitled to it.*[116] Thus parted two lovers, more singular, if not more constant, than perhaps, ever distinguished Columbia's soil.

her I was but a stripling soldier; that I had few talents, and less wealth, to commend me to so much excellence, or even to repay her regard and the favors he had already conferred on me. I told her, moreover, that I was about to rejoin the army, with a view to receive my discharge, and then to return to my relatives in Massachusetts, and to that obscurity from which I had emerged; but I found I had no power to diminish her regard for me.

While taking her hand, as if to bid her a last adieu, I observed in her an indescribable delicacy struggling for expression, and mantling her fine features. Never can I forget the tender yet magnanimous look of disappointment she cast on me, yet without the least tincture of resentment, when, still holding her hand in mine, she replied, that, sooner than wring a reluctant consent from me, she would forego every claim to connubial happiness. But the artless girl continued, if want of wealth on my part were the chief obstacle, I might be relieved from all anxiety on that account, as she was heiress to an ample fortune; it being a legacy which she was to possess on her marriage with a man whose worth should be found in his person rather than in his outward estate. I longed to undeceive her. But the secret I had so long carefully guarded, I could not yet surrender. On parting, she presented me with six fine linen shirts, made with her own hands, an elegant watch, twenty-five Spanish dollars, and five guineas."— MS. Memoir.]

*She has since declared she meant to have executed this resolution, had not some traits of her life been published in the intervening time; and that this lady should have been the first to disclose her sex. Before they parted, she made her a present of six Holland shirts, twenty five guineas and an elegant silver watch. This she will not blush to own, if alive; as it was out of the purest regard for her own sex.

116 "It is no matter how I felt, or what I thought, said, or did on this occasion. I could not, if I would, describe either. I bade her adieu, and staggered to my lodging and to my bed. But, during the greater part of the night, my invocations to 'tired Nature's sweet restorer' were as useless as though 'balmy sleep' were never intended to refresh the exhausted body, or retrieve a bewildered intellect. At length the resolution with which I started when I went to visit my fair friend the day before—to disclose to her the secret of my sex—returned. I knew that this would be right: it was my indispensable duty. On resuming this intention, I fell into a sweet and tranquil slumber." And then she goes on to relate, with great delicacy of manner, and at much length, the interview that occurred at the lady's house that morning, in which the disclosure was fully made, and placed beyond all doubt by an actual inspection. The lady, as may well be supposed, was greatly astonished: reason, for a time, was well-nigh driven from the throne; but the final parting was satisfactory on both sides.

"O Woman! thou bright star of love, whose empire is beauty, virtue, refinement, the world were dark and chaotic without thee. Misanthropy and grossness would characterize man if

This event, as it is unnatural, may be disputed. It is also rare that the same passion should ever have brought a woman to bed with seven children at a birth: And I think eight would rather be miraculous than natural. But it is said, that though perhaps the colouring is a little exaggerated, that this is a fact that will admit of incontestible evidence. Nor need females think themselves piqued to acknowledge it; as no one denies she was not an agreeable object when masqueraded; which, by the by, I am sorry to say, is too often mistaken by that sex.

Thus we have a remarkable instance of the origin of that species of love which renders the enjoyment of life satisfactory, and con summates the bliss of immortality. The passion entertained by the sexes towards each other is doubtless from this source; and will always be laudable, when managed with prudence. But I appeal to the lady's own bosom if after discovering her sister, her passion had not subsided into a calm, and have drooped, like the rose or lily, on its dislocated stalk. About the third of November they arrived at Philadelphia.[117]

left alone; but in thy presence his heart rises to a pure and holy flame. Thy smile is more powerful than the conqueror's sword. Thy sway is mightier than the monarch's sceptre. Thou bindest man as with the sweet influences of a perennial spring."—[*Ibid.*]

117 As Deborah Sampson received her discharge from the army—see in the Introduction her petition to the Legislature of Massachusetts—at West Point, October 25, 1783, here is an evident anachronism in the text.

CHAPTER XII

Doctor Bana (Binney) gives her a letter to Gen. Paterson, then at West Point. On her journey there, she is cast away on Staten Island. The letter discloses her sex to the General. Their interview. She obtains an honorable discharge and recommendations. Goes to her relations in Massachusetts. Intrigues with her sex censured. Reassumes the female attire and economy.

ELATED with her transition from a savage wilderness to a land smiling with agriculture and civilization, her mind was once more illuminated with agreeable prospects. But a review of her situation cast an unfriendly group of objects in her way. A remembrance of the Doctor's queries and injunctions[118] was but recognizing the necessity of a garland of fig leaves to screen a pearl, that could glitter only without disguise.

On the day of her departure from Philadelphia, he entrusted

118 It does not appear what is meant by this. Dr. Binney had always treated her with the greatest delicacy and tenderness.

"On my return to the hospitable mansion of Dr. Binney, in Philadelphia, I told him I had called on him, not to tax his benevolence, which I had already largely experienced, but only to express my gratitude, and to bid him adieu, while hastening to rejoin the army preparatory to my discharge and my return home. Every lineament of his countenance beamed with tenderness and affection as he said, 'I shall insist on your staying with me at least twenty-four hours, as necessary to your rest and refreshment, and as much more time for the expression of the sympathy I feel for you.' Had I met at his house my father and mother, and all my relatives, I could not have felt more at home. The silence that was observed in reference to my sex created doubts in my mind whether the doctor was altogether satisfied with the discovery he had made; and I trembled lest I should be obliged to undergo another personal examination.

When about to depart, the doctor, surrounded by his family, bestowed on me his parting counsels in a manner so tender, that I must have been from that moment a convert to virtue, had I previously been otherwise. In conclusion, he said, 'Take a short prescription as a token of my regard: Be careful of your health, and continue to be as discreet in every thing as you have been true to the cause of freedom; then your country will have a wreath of undying fame for your brow. When you shall have received your discharge from the army, send me a written sketch of your life.' This I partly promised; but, to my shame, I confess that I never fulfilled the promise.

The doctor now put into my hand a large sealed letter, addressed to Gen. Paterson, saying, 'Fail not to deliver this: it contains a bequest for you and for him.' He then, with his whole family, accompanied me to the stage-office, where he had already engaged my passage, and paid the expense of it from Philadelphia to West Point.

About the 12th of October, I arrived at Elizabethtown, in New Jersey."—[MS. Memoir.]

297

her with the care of a letter to Gen. Paterson, then at West Point. Then taking an affectionate farewell of his family, she sat out for the place. She went in the stage to Elizabethtown, 15 miles from New York. The stage boats being gone over, she, with about twelve others went on board the only one remaining. The skipper was reluctant to accompany them, as it was late, rainy and a strong wind ahead. They quickly found the storm increased; and they had not gone half their voyage before they had the terrible prospect of the foundering of a boat with nineteen passengers from South Amboy, bound to New York. Every one was lost. They heard their piteous cries as the surges were closing over their heads; but could afford no relief. Nor was their own prospect much better. It was asked whether it was possible to swim to Staten Island? It was unanimously negatived: but a few minutes put them to the desperate experiment. Being nearly in the centre of the channel, the current rapid, and the storm boisterous, the boat filled with water and sunk under them. Though nothing but death now stared them in the face yet those exertions which had before snatched her from his jaws, we may suppose, were not here unemployed. She had on a large coat, which served to buoy her above the water though she was often ingulphed in the surges. She was washed back twice after reaching the soft sands. But fortunately, clasping her arms on a bed of rushes, she held till many waves had spent their fury over her. Thus recruiting strength, and taking the advantage of the waves, she gained hard bottom and the shore.

On the shore she found others in the same wretched situation, unable to stand. She lay on her face all night. In the morning, the storm having abated, she heard Dr. Vickens say, "Blessed be God, it is day, though I believe I am the only survivor among you all!" Happily, they were all alive except two; who unfortunately found a tomb in the watery element. They were soon taken up by a boat cruising for that purpose, and carried back to Elizabethtown. Most of her equipments, a trunk, including her journal, money, &c., was lost. Her watch and a morocco pocket book, containing the letter, were saved.[119]

The third day, she had a good passage to New York;[120] from thence to West Point. Arrived at the General's quarters she seemed like one sent from the dead; as they had concluded the Potter's Field had long been her home. Her next business was, to deliver the letter. Cruel task! Dreading the contents, she delayed it some days.[121] At length she resolved her fidelity should triumph over every perturbation of mind in the delivery of the letter, and to apologize for her non-trust. Accordingly, finding him alone, she gave him the quivering treasure, made obeisance, turned upon her heel and withdrew in haste.[122]

Precisely an hour after, unattended, he sent for her to his apartment. She says—"A re-entrance was harder than facing a cannonade." Being desired to seat herself, the General, calling her by name, thus gracefully addressed her: "Since you have continued near three years in my service, always vigilant, vivacious, faithful, and, in many respects, distinguished yourself from your fellows, I would only ask—Does that martial attire, which now glitters on your body, conceal a female's form!" The close of the sentence drew tears in his eyes, and she fainted. He used his

119 Mr. Wyatt, a contributor to "Graham's Magazine," says the watch is still in the possession of her descendants. We have the authority of Rev. Mr. Pratt for saying that her canteen, preserved on this occasion, is now in the keeping of a relative of hers at Lakeville, Mass.

120 How could a Continental soldier, in full uniform, be allowed to visit New York, when it was still occupied by the British forces? The British garrison was not withdrawn till November 25, 1783. She certainly did not set foot in New York City at this time.

121 The MS. memoir says she delivered it to him the next morning after her arrival, immediately after breakfast.

122 The MS. memoir contains the letter in full. The letter relates the circumstances of the discovery, made by Dr. Binney in the hospital at Philadelphia, of the sex of the young soldier; speaks very highly and tenderly of the individual; and dwells, at considerable length, on the remarkable features of the case. It is expressed with much delicacy and propriety, and is just such a letter as might have been written by Dr. Binney, a man of benevolent feelings, to Gen. Paterson; and it is certainly a creditable production.

efforts to recover her, which he effected.   But an aspect of wild-
ness was blended in her countenance.   She prostrated herself at
his feet, and begged her life!   He shook his head; but she remembers
not his reply.   Bidding her rise, he gave her the letter, which he
continued to hold in his hand.   Reason having resumed its empire, she read it with emotions.   It was interesting, pathetic and
colored with the pencil of humanity.   He again exclaimed—"Can
it be so!"   Her heart could no longer harbor deception.   Banishing
all subterfuge, with as much resolution, as possible, she confessed
herself—a female.[123]

123 "Attempting to rise from my seat, in order to reply, I lost the control both of body
and mind, and had nearly fainted away.   Recovering, I made out to say, 'What will be my fate,
sir, if I answer in the affirmative?'—'You have nothing to fear,' he replied.   'If you confirm the
statements of this letter,'—still holding the letter of Dr. Binney in his hand,—'you are not only
safe here, but entitled to our warmest respect.'

"'Sir,' I said, 'I am wholly in your power.   God forbid that I should attempt to conceal
what I suppose is now fully known.   I am a Female!   But, oh, sir, now that I am weak and
helpless, withdraw not your protection!'

"'Can it be so?' he exclaimed, after a short pause, as if still in doubt.

"'Sir,' said I, 'I have no desire to deceive you.   Procure for me, if you can, a female
dress,'—an elegant one, I knew, was in the house,—'and allow me a retired place and a half hour
to prepare myself.'

This was immediately complied with          I was completely equipped, from head to
foot, in a lady's attire, within the appointed time . .          Assuming, for the time, some of the
modest, bewitching feminine graces, I returned, and made my *entree* to Gen. Paterson.

The effect was magical.   Never before did I witness ecstasy so complete in man.   'Remain as you are, a short time at least,' said the general.   'This is truly theatrical.   I will summon Jackson, and see if he knows you.'

Col. Jackson was called in, and I was introduced to him as Miss Deborah Sampson.   'She
is from your own State, the cradle of Liberty; and a fit person she is to rock it till the infant is
full grown.   Do you not recognize her?'

'While I should be proud of an acquaintance with such a character, I have no recollection
of this lady,' was the reply.

The conversation then passed to other topics.   At length Gen. Paterson asked if any information respecting Robert Shurtliffe had been received.   'I fear,' said Col. Jackson, 'that
gallant young soldier has fallen a sacrifice to his devotion to liberty.'

'But there are miracles now,—wonders, at least,'—said the general.   'Our Revolution is
full of them.   But this young lady exceeds them all.   Examine her closely, and see if you do not
recognize Robert Shurtliffe!'

Imagination may finish the painting of this scene.   I will add, however, that in this costume I was escorted by these gentlemen over the tented ground, and amidst officers and soldiers, with whom, an hour before, I was as familiar as are the inmates of a family with one another; but none of them knew me."—[MS. Memoir.]

300

He then enquired concerning her relations; but especially of her primeval inducements to occupy the field of war! She proceeded to give a succinct and true account; and concluded by asking, if her life would be spared!—He told her, she might not only think herself safe while under his protection, but that her unrivalled achievements deserved ample compensation—that he would quickly obtain her discharge, and she should be safely conducted to her friends. But having had the tuition of her as a soldier, he said, he must take liberty to give her that advice which he hoped would ornament the functions of her life, when the masculine garb should be laid aside and she taken to the embraces of that sex she was then personating.

Immediately she had an apartment assigned to her own use. And when the General mentioned the event to her Colonel and other officers, they thought he played at cajolery. Nor could they be reconciled to the fact, till it was corroborated by her own words. She requested, as a pledge of her virtue, that strict enquiry should be made of those with whom she had been mess-mate. This was accordingly done.[124] And the effect was—a panic of surprise with every soldier. Groups of them now crowded to behold a phenomenon, which before appeared a natural object. But as access was inadmissible, many turned infidels, and few had faith. Her discharge is from Gen. Knox; her recommendations from the Gens. Paterson and Shepard. *[125]

[124] "Having furnished the gentlemen with an account of my home, my relatives, and the motives which led me to assume the character of a soldier, I requested them to make the strictest inquiry into my manner of life since I had been in the army. This was accordingly done. The result was a general surprise, and, on the part of many, a total disbelief. An apartment was now assigned for my use, and garments for either sex provided. But, in general, I preferred my regimentals, because that in them I should be more safe from insult and annoyance. Many of the soldiers, and many of my own sex, were desirous to satisfy themselves as to the truth of what they had heard; but, of course, it was impossible to gratify their curiosity."

Thus ends Mr. Mann's narrative of the adventures of Deborah Sampson, in which, for the sake of greater force and spirit, the heroine herself is made the speaker.

*Since, by misfortune, lost.

[125] The Definitive Treaty of Peace between Great Britain, France, Spain, and the United

Being informed her effects and diplomas were in readiness, she paid her politest respects to the gentlemen, who accompanied her to the place; and wishing an eternal Farewell to Columbia's Cause, turned her back on the *Aceldama*, once more to re-echo the carols of peace on her native plains.    In the evening, she embarked on board a sloop from Albany to New York: from thence, in Capt. Allen's packet, she arrived at Providence.

Thus she made her exit from the tragic stage.    But how requisite was a parent's house—an asylum from the ebullitions of calumny, where to close the last affecting scene of her complicated, woe-fraught revolution of her sex!    With what eager steps would she have bent her next course over the then congealed glebe—to give a parent the agreeable surprise of beholding her long-lost child —to implore her forgiveness of so wide a breach of duty, and to assume a course of life, which only could be an ornament to her sex and extenuation of her crime!    The ties of consanguinity, of filial

States, was signed at Paris, September 3, 1783.    A state of peace, however, had actually existed in America from the 19th of April, in the same year, when a formal proclamation of the cessation of hostilities was made in the army, by order of the Commander-in-Chief.    Information of the Definitive Treaty having been received, the third day of November was assigned by Congress for disbanding the army of the United States.    The city of New York was evacuated by the British army, November 25.

On the 25th of October, at West Point, our heroine received an honorable discharge from the service from the hand of Gen. Knox.    Many testimonials of faithful performance of duty, and of exemplary conduct in the army, were given to her, among others, from Generals Paterson and Shepard, and Col. Jackson, under whose orders it had been her good fortune to serve. These papers may not have been preserved.

Mrs. Ellet and some others have stated that the commander of the company in which our heroine served, on being informed by Dr. Binney that Robert Shurtliffe was a female, sent the fair soldier with a letter to Gen. Washington, conveying information of the fact; that Washington then gave her a discharge from the army, with a note containing some words of advice, and a sum of money sufficient to bear her expenses home.    A lengthy detail of circumstances is given in connection with this statement.    This account seems to be without any real foundation.    In her petition to the Legislature of Massachusetts, Deborah says she received her discharge from Gen. Knox, as already stated.    Nor is it true, as stated by Mrs. Ellet, that, during the administration of Washington, Deborah received an invitation to visit the seat of Government, and that during her stay, Congress passed an act granting her a pension, in addition to certain lands which she was to receive as a soldier.    No pension was granted her till January 1, 1803, and then not by Act of Congress.    See Introduction, pp. xiii–xvii.

302

affection and of solemn obligation, demanded this. But being deprived of these blessings, she took a few strides to some sequestered hamlet in Massachusetts, where she found some relations: and, assuming the name of her youngest brother, she passed the winter as a man of the world, and was not awkward in the common business of a farmer.[126] But if I remember, she has intimated—that nothing in the villa could have better occupied a greater vacuity, than the diadem—education: which I fondly hope some guardian cherub has since deigned to bestow.

But her correspondence with her sister sex!—Surely it must have been that of sentiment, taste, purity; as animal love, on her part, was out of the question. But I beg excuse, if I happen not to specify every particular of this agreeable round of acquaintance. It may suffice merely to say, her uncle being a compassionate man, often reprehended her for her freedom with the girls of his villa; and them he plumply called fools, (a much harsher name than I can give them) for their violent presumption with the young Continental. Sighing, he would say—their unreserved imprudence would soon detect itself—a multitude of illegitimates!—Columbia would have bewailed the egregious event! Worse, indeed, it might have been, had any one entered against her—not a bill of ejectment, but a system of compulsion, for having won of her a large bet in a

126 About the 1st of November, 1783, she arrived among her relatives in Massachusetts, after an absence of a year and six months. During this period, her information respecting affairs at home had been very limited and vague. Not knowing in what light she might be regarded by those who had formerly known her, she did not immediately discover herself. She still wore her military costume, and did not go to Middleborough, where she had passed most of her life. She went to reside with her uncle in Stoughton, under the assumed name of Ephraim Sampson, that of the younger of her two brothers, if we may trust the statement made in the text. But did not her uncle and his family know that the young soldier who spent the winter with them was not Ephraim Sampson? The supposition is incredible.

The uncle with whom our heroine spent the winter was undoubtedly Mr. Waters, the husband of her mother's sister, Alice Bradford. Sharon was formerly a part of Stoughton. It was during this winter that she became acquainted with her future husband. It is said he was determined to find out whether the newcomer was a man or not, and to some attempt of this nature the next paragraph refers.

She passed the winter doing farm work, and flirting with the girls of the neighborhood.

transport of bliss, after Morpheus had too suddenly whirled away
two-thirds of the night—still refusing to satisfy the demand!—
Blush—blush—rather lament, ye delicate, when so desperate an
extremity is taken to hurl any of your sisters into hymeneal bliss
—wretchedness.

To be plain, I am an enemy to intrigues of all kinds.  Our
female adept had money; and at the worst could have purchased
friends of our sex: But methinks those who can claim the least pre-
tension to feminine delicacy, must be won only by the gentleman,
who can associate the idea of companion without imbibing the
principles of libertinism.  Why did she not, after the crackling
faggot had rivalled the chirping of the cricket in the hearth, caution those, who panted—not like the hunted hart, to taste the
cooling rivulet—that the midnight watch might not have registered
the plighted vows of love!  Having seen the world, and of course
become acquainted with the female heart, and the too fatal avenues to it; why did she not—after convincing them that she lacked
not the courage of a village Hampden, preach to them the necessity
of the prudence and instructions of sage Urania!  That they might
have discovered their weakest place, and have fortified the citadel;
lest a different attack should make a fatal inroad upon their reputation, and transfix a deadly goad through their breasts!  Venus
knows not but she did: but they were all females.

Spring having once more wasted its fragrance from the South,
our heroine leaped from the masculine, to the feminine sphere.[127]

127  On the approach of spring, Deborah resumed feminine apparel and employments.

On the 7th day of April, 1784, she became the wife of Benjamin Gannett, a respectable
and industrious young farmer of Sharon.*  They were married at his father's house in that
town.

*The pedigree of Benjamin Gannett is as follows:—
I.  Matthew Gannett,¹ born in England, 1618, came early to this country, and settled first in Hing-
ham.   In January, 1651-2, he purchased land in Scituate, an adjoining town, and removed to that place.
He died in 1694, as we learn from his grave-stone.   He had several children, of whom Matthew² re-
mained in Scituate, and Rehoboth removed to Morristown, N. J., where he died without'issue.
II.  Joseph Gannett,² son of Matthew,¹ continued to reside in Scituate, and died not long before his
father.   He married a widow Sharp.
III.  Joseph Gannett,³ son of the preceding, removed to East Bridgewater about the year 1722.
His brother Matthew³ removed thither about the same time.  Joseph³ married Hannah Hayward,
daughter of Dea. Jonathan Hayward, of Braintree.  Their son,

Throwing off her martial attire, she once more hid her form with

Her subsequent history must of course have borne a similarity to those of most of our countrywomen who cheer and adorn the homes of New England. She lived to rear a family of reputable children. She had an only son, Capt. Earl B. Gannett, and two daughters. There are grandsons, we believe, now living in Sharon.

She died at her home in Sharon, April 29, 1827, in the sixty-seventh year of her age. She sustained to the end the character of a faithful and exemplary wife and mother, a kind neighbor and friend.

In stature, Deborah Sampson was five feet, seven inches. She was large and full around the waist. Her features were regular, but not beautiful. Her eyes were hazel, inclining to blue; and were lively and penetrating. Her complexion was fair and clear; her aspect was amiable and serene, though somewhat masculine. Her limbs were well proportioned; her movements were quick and vigorous; and her position erect, as became a soldier. Her voice was agreeable;. her speech, deliberate and firm. The portrait at the beginning is from the old copper-plate used at the issue of the *Female Review*, seventy years ago. It was executed when the art of engraving was in its infancy in this country, and must not be supposed to do full justice to the subject.

In military attire, ladies considered her handsome. Several instances are recorded where they were deeply smitten by her good looks. Her delicate appearance, and particularly her having no beard, were often noticed. She was called the "smock-faced boy," and the like; but her sex was never suspected.

The prominent traits of her character were courage, love of adventure, and perseverance under difficulties. She was bold, enterprising, and fearless; she had great self-control, and a firm, resolute will. As a soldier, she exhibited great alertness, activity, fortitude, and valor. Her military life abounded with hardy and hazardous adventures, in all of which she bore herself with the firmness, resolution, and patient endurance which are often thought to belong exclusively to the stronger sex. Where any dared to go, she went; and not to follow merely, but to lead. She often volunteered on expeditions attended with special exposure and hardship. It is said that on scouting parties she would always ride forward a little nearer the enemy than any of her comrades ventured. On one occasion, meeting the enemy suddenly in overwhelming force, it was necessary to abandon their horses, and run across a swamp for dear life. She then showed herself to be as fleet as a gazelle, bounding through the swamp many rods ahead of her companions. It was thought that no man in the army could outrun her.

As we have already seen, she went through two campaigns without the discovery of her sex, and consequently without the loss of her virtue. This fact, which is perfectly well established, demonstrates not only strict moral principle, but the high qualities of firmness, resolution, self-control, and perseverance. Such a case, perhaps, was never known before. It

IV. Benjamin Gannett,[4] born 1728, married, 1750, Mary Copeland, daughter of Jonathan Copeland, of Bridgewater, and removed to Stoughton, the part afterwards Sharon.
V. Benjamin Gannett,[5] born 1753 was the husband of Deborah Sampson, the heroine of our story.
Benjamin Gannett,[4] born 1728, had a brother Joseph,[4] born 1722, who was the father of Caleb Gannett,[5] who was a clergyman in Nova Scotia, afterwards tutor in Harvard College, and for many years steward of the institution. Caleb Gannett[5] married a daughter of Rev. Ezra Stiles, D.D., President of Yale College. They were the parents of Rev. Ezra Stiles Gannett, D.D., of Boston.
Joseph Gannett,[3] who settled in East Bridgewater about 1722, had by a second wife, Hannah Brett, a son Matthew,[4] born 1755, who was the father of Rev. Allen Gannett, late of Lynnfield, now of Boston. —[*Mitchell's Bridgewater*.]

## the dishabille of Flora, recommenced her former occupation; and I

certainly stood alone in the Revolutionary war.  She was never found in liquor,—a vice too common in all armies.  It is well known that the Continental army, though composed in an unusual degree of men of principle and virtue, contained many men of unsound character.  No stain appears to have attached to the character of our heroine.

To gratify the curiosity of the multitude, she once visited Boston; and in the theatre, clad in military attire, she went through, at the word of a military officer, the manual exercise.  Those who witnessed the performance said that "she would almost make the gun talk;" every time it came to the ground from her hand, the sound was so significant.

Her deportment was eminently soldier-like, and none were more expert in the drill than herself.  Mr. Amos Sampson, who is now living in Charlestown at the age of nearly seventy-nine, told me that he witnessed the scene, and that it occurred when he was an apprentice to the printing-business, and therefore between 1801 and 1808.  He said, moreover, that it was in the theatre, and not on the Common, as has been elsewhere represented.

It appears that the remarkable story of Deborah Sampson began to be bruited abroad very soon after her discharge from the army, before her marriage with Mr. Gannett, and even before her relinquishment of military costume.  The Appendix will contain a notice of this singular case, as it was published in a New York paper, and afterwards copied into some papers in Massachusetts.  The principal facts in her career were thus published to the world in a little more than two months after her discharge from the army.  These facts could only have been derived from the officers to whom the disclosure was originally made; perhaps from Gen. Paterson himself.  The facts were so remarkable, that there was a strong inducement to give them to the public.  Their publication in Massachusetts must have awakened inquiry respecting the heroine, and perhaps led the way to her disclosing the whole story to the author of the *Female Review*.

Immediately following the extract to which we have just referred, is the certificate of Col. Henry Jackson, which further authenticates the case.  A certified copy of it is on file in the office of the Secretary of the Commonwealth.

The following notice of Deborah Sampson appeared in print several years before her death.  It is taken from the *Dedham Register* of December, 1820, and was copied into many of the papers of the day:—

"We were much gratified to learn that during the sitting of the court in this town the past week, Mrs. Gannett, of Sharon, in this county, presented for renewal her claims for services rendered her country as a soldier in the Revolutionary army.  The following brief sketch, it is presumed, will not be uninteresting: This extraordinary woman is now in the sixty-second year of her age: she possesses a clear understanding, and a general knowledge of passing events; is fluent of speech, and delivers her sentiments in correct language, with deliberate and measured accent; is easy in her deportment, affable in her manners, robust and masculine in her appearance.  She was about eighteen years of age when our Revolutionary struggle commenced.  The patriotic sentiments which inspired the heroes of those days, and urged them to battle, found their way to a female bosom.  The news of the carnage which had taken place on the plains of Lexington had reached her dwelling; the sound of the cannon at the battle of Bunker Hill had vibrated on her ears; yet, instead of diminishing her ardor, it only served to increase

306

know not, that she found difficulty in its performance. Whether her enthusiasm in the sacred cause of liberty, in which she beheld her country engaged. She privately quitted her peaceful home and the habiliments of her sex, and appeared at the head-quarters of the American army as a young man, anxious to join his efforts to those of his coun-trymen in their endeavors to oppose the inroads and encroachments of the common enemy. She was received and enrolled in the army by the name of Robert Shurtliffe. For the space of three years, she performed the duties, and endured the hardships and fatigues of a soldier; during which time, she gained the confidence of her officers, by her expertness and precision in the manual exercise, and by her exemplary conduct. She was a volunteer in several hazar-dous enterprises, and was twice wounded by musket balls. So well did she contrive to conceal her sex, that her companions in arms had not the least suspicion that the "blooming soldier" fighting by their side was a female; till at length a severe wound, which she received in battle, which had well-nigh closed her earthly career, occasioned the discovery. On her recovery, she quitted the army, and became intimate in the families of Gen. Washington and other dis-tinguished officers of the Revolution. A few years afterwards, she was married to her present husband, and is now the mother of several children. Of these facts there can be no doubt. There are many living witnesses in this county, who recognized her on her appearance at court, and were ready to attest to her services. We often hear of such heroines in other countries but this is an instance in our own country, and within the circule of our acquaintance."

It will be observed that the foregoing account confirms and authenticates the general state-ment made in this volume. There are some errors of detail, which might easily creep into an account like this, where perfect accuracy was not demanded. The statement that Mrs. Gan-nett served three years as a soldier, originated, no doubt, from the fact that she enlisted for three years, though her actual length of service was much less.

Under date of June 25, 1859, Rev. Stillman Pratt, of Middleborough, who had become in-terested in her history writes:—

"In my recent visit to Sharon, I spent some time at the residence and by the grave of Mrs. Deborah Gannett, formerly Deborah Sampson. The house was built by Mrs. Gannett, her husband, and his only son, about fifty years ago, with brick ends, the residue of wood. It is two stories high. The western portion is literally embowered with willow-trees, one of which was set out by Deborah herself, and now measures twelve feet in circumference, and almost constitutes a grove of itself. The eastern portion is covered by a woodbine, which extends over the roof, and climbs to the top of the chimney. Rose bushes and other flowering shrubs are interspersed with perennial plants. The barn stands directly back of the house; in the rear of which rises a sugar loaf mound, of peculiar aspect, extending back towards a dense forest.

The farm consists of a hundred acres of land, with every possible variety of soil. The mowing lands are irrigated by artificial streams of water, branching off in all directions, and discharging themselves into a small river below. In the hedges, and along the walls, are rasp-berry and barberry bushes; while fruit and shade trees are promiscuously mingled through the fields.

One mile south of this residence is located the old cemetery. On the tenth row from the entrance are three plain slate-stone slabs, commemorative of the last resting-place of Mr. and Mrs. Gannett, and of Capt. Earl B. Gannett, their only son."

this was done voluntarily, or compulsively, is to me an enigma. But she continues a phenomenon among the revolutions of her sex.

A friend of the publishers of this volume has lately visited the spot, and has enabled them to furnish the representation of these funeral monuments, which will be found on the following leaf.

After Mrs. Gannett's death, the following notice appeared in 'Niles's Weekly Register,''' vol. xxxii., p. 217, Baltimore, May 26, 1827:—

"A Female Veteran.—The *Dedham Register* states that Mrs. Deborah Gannett, wife of Mr. Benjamin Gannett, of Sharon, Mass., died on the 19th [29th] ult. She enlisted as a volunteer in the American army of the Revolution, in the Massachusetts corps, having the dress and appearance of a soldier. She continued in the service until the end of the war, three years, sustaining an unsullied character, and performing the duties of a soldier with more than ordinary alertness and courage, having been twice dangerously wounded; though she preserved her sex undiscovered. At the disbanding of the army, she received an honorable discharge, and returned to her relatives in Massachusetts, still in her regimentals. When her case was made known to the government of that State, her full wages were paid, and a considerable bounty added. Congress allowed her a pension, which she regularly received. Soon after she resumed the sphere of her own sex, she was married to Mr. Gannett, an industrious, respectable farmer. She was borne and reared him a reputable family of children; and to the close of life she has merited the character of an amiable wife, a tender mother, a kind and exemplary neighbor, and a friend of her country.

Mr. H. Mann, of Dedham, published a memoir of her life some time since, of which the whole edition, 1,500 copies, has been entirely sold. Another edition may be soon expected, enlarged and improved, which will probably meet a rapid sale."

This obituary notice was undoubtedly written by Mr. Mann himself; who, if not the editor, was, I believe, a principal contributor to the *Dedham Register* at that time. Some of the expressions in this obituary notice, used in summing up her character, are identical with some which are employed for the same purpose in the MS. memoir, from which I have so often quoted. And this very MS. memoir, now in my possession, is, beyond question, the document referred to in the last sentence quoted above from the *Register*.

The publishers of the present edition having determined to issue an exact reprint of the *Female Review*, it was a matter of necessity to reproduce every sentence and every expression, however faulty in point of taste, and objectionable in respect of moral sentiment. There are many passages, there are entire paragraphs, which the present editor would gladly have omitted. Many expressions are awkward and ungainly, and do not truly represent the author's own meaning. For the insertion of such passages, the editor must not be held responsible. To have attempted any thing in the way of counteraction would have been worse than useless.

The editor is of opinion that Deborah Sampson was worthy of an abler biographer than she found in the original compiler, and that her adventures, which were certainly very remarkable, were worthy of being related in far better style.                          J. A. V.

Boston, July, 1866.

APPENDIX

# APPENDIX

AFTER delineating the life of a person, it seems natural to recapitulate, in a closer assemblage, the leading features of his character.

Perhaps a spirit of enterprize, perseverance and competition was never more distinguishable in a female, than in Miss Sampson. And whilst we are surprised that she left her own tranquil sphere for the most perilous—the field of war, we must acknowledge it is at least, a circumstantial link in the chain of our illustrious revolution. She never would accept a promotion while in the army; though it is said she was urged to take a Lieutenant's commission.

I will here give an instance of her dread of rivalship. It was soon after she inlisted. Having been reluctantly drawn into a ring of wrestling, she was worsted; though it is said, she flung a number. But the idea of a competitor deprived her of sleep the whole night. Let this be a memento to Columbia's daughters; that they may beware of too violent scuffles with our sex. We are athletic, haughty and unconquerable. Besides, your dislocated limbs are a piteous sight! And it seems this was a warning to her: for it was noted by the soldiers, that she never wrestled, nor suffered any one to twine his arms, about her shoulders, as was their custom when walking.

And lest her courage has not been sufficiently demonstrated, I will adduce one more instance, that must surpass all doubt. In 1782, she was sent from West Point, on business, to a place called the Clove, back of the high hills of Santee.* She rode Capt. Phelon's horse. On her return, just at the close of twilight, she was

*A most singular blunder—these "Hills" are in South Carolina.

311

surprised by two ruffians, who rushed hastily from a thicket, seized her horse's bridle, and demanded her money, or her life.  She was armed with a brace of pistols and a hanger.  Looking at the one, who held the horse, she said, "F. B.———, I think I know you; and this moment you become a dead man, if you persist in your demand!"  Hearing a pistol cock at the same time, his compeer fled; and he begged quarter and forgiveness; which she granted, on condition of a solemn promise ever to desist from so desperate an action.

It is perhaps sufficiently authenticated, that she preserved her chastity by a rare assiduity to conceal her sex.  Females can best conceive inconveniences to which she was subject.  But as I know not that she ever gratified any one with the wondrous *éclaircisse ment*, I can only say, perhaps, what more have heard than ex perienced—"Want prompts the wit, and first gave birth to arts." If it be true, and if—"a moment of concealment is a moment of humiliation," as an anonymous writer of her sex observes, she has humility enough to bow to the shrine of modesty, and to appear without disguise, from top to toe.

Since writing these sheets, I have been pained for a few, especially females, who seem unwilling to believe that a female went through three campaigns without the discovery of her sex, and consequently, the loss of virgin purity.*

We hear but little of an open prostitute in the army, or elsewhere—of Collin and Dolly, the milk maid, in their evening saunter ing to the meadow.  Then why should any be so scrupulous of her, because she did not go in the professed character of a soldier's trull! Though it is said she was an uncommonly modest soldier; yet, like you, I am ready to aver she has made a breach in female delicacy.

*"She had no beard," is an objection, to which I know not that this class of readers can be reconciled.—A chaplain, since known in Massachusetts, was once at Gen. Paterson's quarters.  In the presence of his smock-faced attendant, he took occasion to compliment the General—"I admire your fare; but nothing more than you very polite attendant, who appears to possess the graceful activity and bloom of a girl."

But bring forth her fallacious pretensions to virtue; and I am bound, as a moralist, to record them—as vices, to be guarded against.    I have only to desire this class of my readers to think as favorable as possible of our sex; but on all accounts to cherish the lovely fugitive—virtue, in their own.    For too much suspicion of another's, argues too strongly a want of the same charming ornament in themselves; unless they are old maids, or bachelors.

I shall here make a small digression.    As our heroine was walking the streets in Philadelphia, in a beautiful, serene evening, she was ravished by the sweet, pensive notes of a *piano-forte*. Looking up at a third loft she discovered a young female, who seemed every way expressive of the music she made.    She often after listened to the same sounds; and was as often surprised that a sigh should be blended with such exquisite harmony and beauty.    Of this female, I will transmit to my readers the following pathetic history.

Fatima was the eldest of three daughters, whose parents had acquired an ample fortune, and resided in a part of the United States where nature sheds her blessings in profuse abundance. But unhappily, their conduct towards them was distinguished, like that of others, whose fondness so infinitely exceed their prudence. They were not, however, deficient in many external accomplishments.    Early was Fatima taught to speak prettily, rather than properly; to admire what is brilliant, instead of what is solid; to study dress and pink à la mode; to be active at her toilet, and much there; to dance charmingly at a ball, or farcical entertainment; to form hasty and miscellaneous connexions; to show a beautiful face, and sigh for admiration;—in short, to be amused, rather than instructed; but at last—to discover an ill accomplished mind!    This is beauty in a maze.    Such occupations filled up her juvenile years. Her noblest proficiencies were music, drawing, &c. but an injudicious choice of books excluded their influence, if they had any, from her mind.    Thus we may conclude her course of education led her to set the greatest estimate on this external new kind of creature; whilst her internal source—her immortal part, remained, as in a fog, or like a gem in a tube of adamant.

Nature had been lavish in the formation of Fatima. And on her first appearance, one must have been strongly impressed in her favor. But what says the sequel?—The invigorating influence of Venus had scarcely warmed her bosom, when towards the close of a beautiful, soft day, in her rural excursion, she first beheld Philander who had become a gleaner in her father's fields. A mutual impulse of passions, till then unfelt, fired their bosoms: for Philander was much indebted to nature for a polished form; and something uncommonly attracting in his looks seemed to veil the neglect of his mind. Unfortunate youth! His parents were poor: and to add to his misery, they had deprived him of their only, and yet most important, legacy—I mean, the cultivation of his mind. Had not this been his lot, he might have made himself rich and Fatima happy.

After this, Fatima's chief delight was to walk in the fields, to see her father's flock, and to listen to the pipe of Philander. Repeated interviews brought them more acquainted with each other. Each attempted to steal the lustre of the eye and the crimson blush, which a too warm constitution could ill conceal. At length, an unreserved familiarity took place. Both had been taught to love; and both had missed Plato's and Urania's system, which should have taught them—how. Fatima durst not let her parents know that a peasant possessed her virginal love. She therefore, under pretence of regaling herself in the garden, often reserved the keys that secured its avenues: and whilst the dew distilled its pensive sweets, the sequestered alcove, or embowered grass plat, too often witnessed their lambent amours.

One night—a night that must ever remain horrible to their remembrance, and which should be obliterated from the annals of time—Fatima sat at the window of her apartment, to behold, rather than contemplate, the beauties of the evening. The hamlet was at rest, when she discovered Philander passing in the street. Her dishabille too plainly disclosed her charms, when she hastened with the fatal key to the garden gate, where Philander had just arrived. The massy door having grated upon its hinges, they walked a number of times through the bowling-green, till at length, almost imperceptibly, they found themselves at the door, that led to Fatima's apartment. The clock struck twelve, when they tip-toed through a number of windings, till they arrived at the chamber; which, till then, had been an asylum for the virginity of Fatima.

It is needless to paint the scenes that succeeded. A taper she had left burning on her 'scrutoire, with the rays of the moon, reflected a dim light on the rich furniture of the room and on the alcove in which lay, for the last time, the tranquil Fatima! But this light, feeble as it was disclosed to Philander a thousand new charms in the fascinating spectacle of so much love and beauty. Sensuality took the lead of every reasoning faculty; and both became instrumental to their own destruction. Philander became a total slave to his passions. He could no longer revere the temple of chastity. He longed to erect his fatal triumph on the ruins of credulous virtue. He saw nothing but what served to inflame his passions. His eyes rioted in forbidden delights. And his warm embraces kindled new fires in the bosom of this beauteous maid. The night was silent as death: not a zephyr was heard to rustle in the leaves below—but Heaven was a recording witness to their criminal pleasures!

The lost Fatima beheld her brutal ravisher with horror and distraction. But from that fatal moment, his enthusiastic love cooled; and he shunned her private recesses and public haunts. Fatima, to avoid the indignation of her parents, eloped from them. Her eyes were opened! Many were her wearisome steps to find an asylum from that guilt, which, through her parents' neglect, she incurred on herself. In vain did she lament that some piteous cherub had not preserved her to a more propitious fate—that she had not been doomed to a cloistered convent, to have made an eternal vow of celibacy, to have prostrated herself to wooden statues, to have kissed the feet of monks and to have pined away her life in solitude! Thus she continues to mourn the loss of that happiness she lost through neglect of education.

Fatima was in her female attire—our heroine was a soldier. And I should sacrifice many tender feelings to prefer to my Fair readers—the situation of either.

I confess, I might justly be thought a monster to the female sex, were I willing to suggest that her original motive was the company of the venal sycophant, the plotting knave, the disgusting, ugly debauchee: or that her turning volunteer in Columbia's cause was a meditated plot against her own sex. Oh! this would be too cruel. Custom is the dupe of fancy: nor can we scarcely conceive what may not be relished, till the fugitive has worn out every shift. But let us remember, though it constitutes our esteem and reverence, it does not, always, our prudence and propriety. A high cut robe, for instance, though it may agreeably feast the imagination, may not prove the most prudent garb for every fair object, who wears it. But in the asylum of female protection, may I not be thought their meanest votary, should not a humble ejaculation prevent every robe-wearer from being led

"O'er infant innocence—to hang and weep,
Murder'd by ruffian hands—when smiling in its sleep!"

It need not be asked whether a proper union of the sexes is recommendable and just. Nature claims this as her primogenial and indissoluble bond and national custom establishes the mode. But to mention the intercourse of our heroine with her sex, would, like others more dangerous, require an apology I know not how to make. It must be supposed, she acted more from necessity than a voluntary impulse of passion; and no doubt, succeeded beyond her expectations, or desires. Harmless thing! An useful veteran in war! An inoffensive companion in love! These are certainly requisites, if not virtues. They are always the soldier's glory; but too seldom his boast. Had she been capacitated and inclined to prey, like a vulture, on the innocence of her sex, vice might have hurried vice, and taste have created appetition. Thus she would have been less entitled to the clemency of the public. For individual crimes bring on public nuisances and calamities and debauchery is one of the first. But incapacity, which seldom begets desire, must render her in this respect unimpeachable.

Remember, females, I am your advocate; and like you would pay my devoirs to the Goddess of love. Admit that you conceived an attachment for a female soldier. What is the harm? She acted in the department of that sex whose embraces you naturally seek. From a like circumstance we are liable to the same impulse. Love is the ruling dictate of the soul. But viewing Venus in all her influential charms—did she gain too great an ascendancy over that virtue, which should guard the receptacle of your love? Did the dazzling enchantress, after fascinating you in her wilds, inhumanly leave you in a situation—ready to yield the pride and ornament of your sex—your white-robed innocence a sacrifice to lawless lust and criminal pleasure! I congratulate the fair object, whoever she was, and rejoice with her most sincerely, that she happily mistook the ferocity of the lion, for the harmlessness of the lamb! You have thus wonderfully escaped the fatal rock on which so many of both sexes (it wounds me to repeat it!) have made shipwreck of this inestimable prize. You have thus preserved inviolate your coronet of glory, your emblematic diadem of innocence, friendship, love, and beauty—the pride of your sex—the despair and envy of the dissolute incendiary! This is your virginity—that chastity which is such an additional ornament to beauty.

The sun, with all his *éclat*, which has so often gone down on your innocence, shall continue to rise with increasing beauty, and give you fresh satisfaction and delight. Taunt, invective and calumny may storm and, tho' you may dread, you may defy, their rage. But what will be a still greater source of comfort, old reflection shall not awfully stare you in the face on your bridal day: nor remorse steal an imperceptible course into your bosoms; nor, as with the scorpion's dagger, wound your tenderest place. Instead of a girdle of thorns, the amaranthine wreath shall encircle you, and the banners of friendship, love and tranquillity shall ever hover over you. Whilst others, guilty of a breach in this emblem of paradise, may escape with impunity the deserved lash of aspersion from a chaste husband (for there may be chaste men as well as chaste women), you shall be presented to your partner of life, an object uncontaminated from the hands of your Creator. And next to the Giver of all good, he shall extatically hold you in his embraces, and esteem you as the object of his supreme affections.

As the pure and brilliant dew-drop on the rose and lilly gathers their fragrance; as the surface of the limpid stream outspreads its azure flow for curious investigation so, shall your words and actions be received by all who are round about you. Your children, as coming from an unpolluted source, shall rise up and call you blessed. And whilst the dupe and rude in thought shall deign to bow at your shrine, your worth shall daily be enhanced in your husband's estimation. He shall not forget to heap encomiums on your merit, when he sits among the primogeniture of the land. A mutual exchange and increase of affection will be perpetuated to you, through a long series of satisfactory enjoyments—even till second childishness steals upon you, and till time itself dissolves your earthly compact, and seals you in the dust. Heaven, the residentiary mansion of bliss for the faithful and pure, will, at last, condescend to crown you with a rich reward for your services, for your integrity and virtue. Females, Adieu!

Columbia demands our review. To stretch the memory

318

to the momentous Epoch, when the optics of sage Columbus first lighted on the American shores, and to trace the mazy clue of her annals from a savage wilderness to the present period, when she stand confessed, a new star among the nations of the earth—an Elysian field of beauty, must feast the intellectual system with every idea, perhaps of pain and pleasure. When we remember the sweat of the brow in the culture of her once stubborn glebe, our encounters with the tomahawk, and with the more formidable weapons of death in our late revolution, the breast must be callous to sensation, that does not own the privileges and felicity to which we are now exalted have been bought at a rate dear enough to be instructive.

We have moulded a constitutional government, at our option. It also guarantees to us the privilege of making amendments: and under its continued auspices, what good may we not anticipate? Scarcely three hundred years have rolled away, since America was a solitary haunt for savages and beasts. But behold now, under the fostering hands of industry and economy, how she smiles; even from the magnificence of the city, passing the pleasant country villas, to the moss-covered cot! The sun of science is gleaming on her remotest corners; and his penetrating rays are fast illuminating the whole empire of reason. Hail, then, thou happy, radiant source of beauty!—Our progress has indeed been rapid: heaven grant it may be lasting.

O war, thou worst of scourges! Whilst we hear of thy depredations, which are now laying Europe in blood and ashes—indeed Columbia, we think of you! And is there any who are ignorant of the horrors of war, and thirst for the gratification? Let such be cautious of their propensities. You have heard, I suppose, that an Emperor, Cardinal, or a gracious, sable-headed Pope, has issued an edict, laying claim to a certain territory, to which, nobody ever mistrusted he was entitled. But the nation has turned infidels to his creed; and though he is a man of insult, he is not to be insulted.

He collects his forces, and marches to glory; kills millions, gains his conquest, renews his quarrels and puts others to the sword. His men are called veterans! What are ours called?—A youth, a female, a young nymph may tell.

And must the scourge of war again cast a gloom over Columbia's beauteous surface? Must infernal furies from distant regions conspire her ruin? Shall her own sons, forgetful of that happiness they have purchased so dearly, unmindful of an infinite variety of alluring objects that surround them, grow wanton in luxury and indolence, and thirst, like tygers, to imbrue their hands in the blood of any of the human race? God forbid! For in that day the beast shall again retire to his lair; the bird shall clap its well-fledged wing, and bear itself across the ocean; (Heaven grant it there may have a chance to land)! and the fish shall lie in torpitude, or refuse the angler's bait—but all, looking up to that sublime and exalted creature, Man, bewail the time he had rule given over them!

But, Columbia, this must never be said of your progeny. It has been necessary they should encounter the bitters—the calamities of war. It now remains, that they taste and long preserve the sweets of prosperity. The sylvan bard shall compose for you, his canzonets and roundelays, and the minstrel shall rehearse them to his tranquil audience, in your silent, green-wood shade. From the city, the sailor shall quit your beauteous shores with reluctance and with a sigh. And while old ocean is heaving his barque from his home, as your lessening turrets bluely fade to his view, he shall climb the mast—and while he is snatching a fond review, reflection shall feast his memory with every pleasurable and pensive sensation. And though separated from his natal clime by oceans, climes and nations, his choicest hopes and wishes shall dwell in his native land.

It remains to authenticate the facts asserted.  The following first appeared in a New York paper, from which it was copied in others, in Massachusetts:

## New York, January 10, 1784.

An extraordinary instance of virtue in a Female Soldier has lately occurred, in the American army, in the Massachusetts line, viz. a lively, comely young nymph, nineteen years of age, dressed in man's apparel, has been discovered; and what redounds to her honor, she has served in the character of a soldier for nearly three years, undiscovered.  During this time, she displayed much alertness, chastity and valor: having been in several engagements, and received two wounds—a small shot remaining in her to this day. She was a remarkable, vigilant soldier on her post; always gained the applause of her officers—was never found in liquor, and always kept company with the most temperate and upright soldiers.  For several months, this Gallantress served, with credit, in a General Officer's family.  A violent illness, when the troops were at Philadelphia, led to the discovery of her sex.  She has since been honorably discharged from the Army, with a reward,* and sent to her connexions; who, it appears, live to the Eastward of Boston, at a place, called Meduncook.

The cause of her personating a man, it is said, proceeded from the rigor of her parents, who exerted their prerogative to induce her marriage with a young gentleman, against whom she had conceived a great antipathy; together with her being a remarkable heroine and warmly attached to the cause of her country, in the service of which, it must be acknowledged, she gained reputation; and no doubt, will be noticed in the history of our grand revolution.  She passed by the name of Robert Shurtliffe while in the army, and was borne on the rolls as such.  For particular reasons, her name is witheld: But the facts, above mentioned, are unquestionable and unblemished.

*This she has not received.  EDITOR.  [H. Mann.]

Boston, August 1, 1786.

To all whom it may concern.

These may certify, that Robert Shurtliffe was a Soldier in my Regiment, in the Continental Army, for the town of Uxbridge in the Commonwealth of Massachusetts, and was inlisted for the term of three years—that he had the confidence of his officers, did his duty, as a faithful and good Soldier, and was honorably discharged the Army of the United States.

HENRY JACKSON, *late Col. in the American Army.*

RESOLVE *of the* GENERAL COURT—*January* 20, 1792.

On the petition of Deborah Gannet, praying compensation for services performed in the late Army of the United States:

WHEREAS it appears to this Court, that the said Deborah Gannet inlisted under the name of Robert Shurtliffe, in Capt. Webb's company in the fourth Massachusetts regiment, on May 21, 1782, and did actually perform the duties of a soldier, in the late Army of the United States, to the 23d day of October, 1783; for which she has received no compensation. And whereas it further appears, that the said Deborah exhibited an extraordinary instance of female heroism, by discharging the duties of a faithful, gallant soldier; and at the same time, preserved the virtue and chastity of her sex, unsuspected and unblemished, and was discharged from the service, with a fair and honorable character.

Therefore, resolved, that the Treasurer of this Common wealth be, and hereby is directed to issue his note, to said Deborah, for the sum of thirty-four pounds, bearing interest from October 23, 1783.

As it is nothing strange that any girl should be married, and have children; it is not to be expected, that one, distinguished like Miss Sampson, should escape. The greatest distinction lies in the qualification for this important business. And, perhaps, the greatest requisite for Education is—complete union with the parties, both in theory and practice. This is remarkably verified in the party spirits that bring on wars and public calamities. They extend to the remote fireside.

It is hearsay, that Mrs. Gannet refuses her husband the rites of the marriage bed. She must, then, condescend to smile upon him in the silent alcove, or grass plat; as she has a child, that has scarcely left its cradle. It is possible, she experiences, not only corporal but mental inabilities; and in mercy to her generation, would keep it in non-existence. But this is not the part of a biographer. I am sorry to learn, this is mostly female complaint, and not authentic, for her nearest neighbors assert there is a mutual harmony subsisting between her and her companion; which, by the bye, is generally the reverse with those deprived of this hymeneal bliss. All who are acquainted with her must acknowledge her complaisant and humane dispositions. And while she discovers a taste for an elegant stile of living; she exhibits, perhaps, an unusual degree of contentment, with an honest farmer, and three endearing children, confined to a homely cot and a hard-earned little farm.

She is sometimes employed in a school in her neighborhood. And her first maxim of the government of children is implicit obedience. I cannot learn, she has the least wish to usurp the prerogatives of our sex. For she has often said, that nothing appears more beautiful in the domestic round than when the husband takes the lead, with discretion, and is followed by his consort, with an amiable acquiescence. She is, however, of opinion, that those women, who threaten their children with, "I will tell your father"—of a crime they should correct, is infusing into them a spirit of triumph they should never know. The cultivation of humanity and good nature is the grand business of education. And she has seen the ill effects of fighting, enough to know the necessity of sparing clubs

and cuffs at home. The same good temper we would form in our
offspring, should be exhibited in ourselves. We should neither use
our children as strangers; nor as the mere tools of fanciful sport.
All tampering and loose words with them, are, like playing careless-
ly with the lion or tiger, who will take advantage of our folly. In
short, instructions should be infused, as the dew distils; and discipline, neither rigid, nor tyrannic, should rest, like a stable pillar.

How great—how sacred are our obligations to our offspring!
Females, who are the the vehicles by which they are brought into
the world, cannot consider, too seriously the subject. Let it not
be delayed, then, till that love, which coalesces the sexes, produces
an object for experiment. Form a pre-affection for the sweet innocent, while in embryo—that it may be cherished, with prudence,
when brought to view. And may we never have it to lament—
that while any females contemplate, with abhorrence, a female,
who voluntarily engages in the field of battle—they forget to recoil
at the idea of coming off victorious from battles, fought by their
own domestic—firesides! We have now seen the distinction of one
female. May it stimulate others to shine—in the way, that Virtue prescribes.

THE END.

### A

Rev. David Avery, Wrentham.
Col. Philip Ammidon, Mendon.
Mr. Benjamin Allen, R. I. College.
  Armand Auboyneau, Do.
  Jason Abbot, Boylston.
  Oliver Adams, Milford.
  John Whitefield Adams, Medfield.
  John Wickliffe Adams, Do.
  Charles Aldrich, Mendon.
  Ahaz Allen, Do.
  Seth Allen, Sharon.

### B

Moses Bullen, Esq. Medfield.
Maj. Noah Butterworth, Wrentham.
Capt. Eli Bates, Bellingham.
Doct. Thomas Bucklin, Hopkinton.
Mr. Nicholas Bowen, Merchant, Providence.
  George Benson, Do. Do.
  Liberty Bates, R. I. College.
  John Baldwin, Do.
  Lemuel Le Bararon, Do.
  Allen Bourn, Do.
  Horatio G. Brown, Do.
  Joseph Brown, Byfield.
  Jason Babcock, Dedham.
  Eli Blake, Wrentham.
  Isaac Bennett, Do.
  David Blake, Do.
  Henry S. Bemis, Stoughton.
  George Boyd, Boston.
  Amos Boyden, Medfield.
  Baruch Bullard, Uxbridge.
  Ebenezer Bugbee, Roxbury.

### C

Mr. Nathan Cary, R. I. College.
  Judah A. McClellen, Do.
  Gaius Conant, Do.
  Joseph B. Cook, Do.
  Asa Cheney, Milford.

Ichabod Corbett, Do.
Luther Cobb, Bellingham.
John Cobb, Wrentham.
Joseph Cleavland, Do.
Joseph Cleale, Byfield.
Jabez Chickering, jun. Dedham.
Winsow Corbett, Mendon.
George Crane, Stoughton.
Joseph Curtis, Roxbury.
Calvin Curtis, Sharon.

### D

Capt. Isaac Doggett, Dedham.
Lieut. Samuel Day, Wrentham.
Mr. Andrew Dexter, jun. R. I. College.
  Paul Dodge, R. I. College.
  James Dupee, Walpole.
  Joseph Daniels, Merchant, Franklin.
  John Dummer, Byfield.

### E

Capt. Amos Ellis, Bellingham.
Mr. Samuel Ervin, R. I. College.
  James Ervin, Do.
  John Ellis, Dedham.
  Aaron Ellis, Walpole.
  Asa Ellis, jun. Brookfield.
  Ebenezer Estee, Milford.
  Samuel Elliot, Byfield.

### F

Hon. Timothy Farrar, New Ipswich.
  Amariah Frost, Esq. Milford.
Lieut. Samuel Fuller, Walpole.
Mr. Theodore D. Foster, R. I. College.
  Drury Fairbanks, Do.
  Ebenezer Fales, Walpole.
  Suel Fales, Do.
  Shubael Fales, Do.
  Elijah Fisher, Sharon.
  Ebenezer Foster, Wrentham.
  William B. Fisher, Do.

325

### G

Rev. Thomas Gray, Roxbury.
David S. Grenough, Esq. Do.
Mr. William Green, R. I. College.
Mr. Franklin Green, R. I. College.
Isaac Greenwood, Providence.
Otis Greene, Mendon.
Joseph Gay, Wrentham.
Ephraim Grove, Bridgewater.
John Green, Medway.
Miss Susanna Gay, Wrentham.

### H

Alexander Hodgdon, Esq. Dedham.
Maj. Samuel Hartshorn, Walpole.
Mr. John P. Hitchcock, R. I. College.
Washington Hathaway, Do.
Samuel Hayward, Milford.
Nathan Hawes, Wrentham.
David Hartwell, Stoughton.

### I

Mr. Thomas P. Ives Merchant, Providence
James Jones, Byfield.
Phinehas Johnson, R. I. College.
Jesse Joslin, Thompson.

### K

Mr. Richard King, Byfield.
Asa Kingsbury, Franklin.
Ambrose Keith, Northbridge.

### L

Mr. Grant Learned, Boston.
Laban Lewis, Stoughton.
Miss Alice Leavens, Walpole.

### M

Col. Timothy Mann, Walpole.
Sabin Mann, Medfield.
Capt. Daniel Morse, Brookfield.
Mr. William P. Maxwell, R. I. College.
Elias Mann, Northampton.
Windsor Mainard, Mendon.
Paul Moody, Byfield.
John Messinger, jun. Wrentham.
David Moores, Byfield.
Lewis Miller, Dedham.

### N

Mr. John Nelson, Merchant, Milford.

### O

Mr. Nathaniel G. Olney, R. I. College.
Miss Hannah Orne, Boston.

### P

Doctor Elias Parkman, Milford, 6 copies.
Capt. Abijah Pond, Wrentham.
Deac. Jacob Pond, Do.
Mr. Eleazar Perry, Merchant, Hopkinton.
Samuel Penniman, Milford.
Josiah Penniman, Mendon.
Baruch Penniman, Do.
Abiel Pettee, Dedham.
Adam Ward Partridge, Chesterfield.

### R

Benjamin Randall, Esq. Sharon.
John M. Roberts, A. B. R. I. College.
Mr. John Rogers, Merchant, Cumberland.
James Reed, Stoughton.

### S

Seth Smith, jun. Esq. Norton, 6 Copies.
Ebenezer Seaver, Esq. Roxbury.
Capt. John Soule, Middleborough, 6 Copies.
Mr. John Sabin, R. I. College.
John Simmons, Do.
William H. Sabin, Do.
Jonas Smith, Rutland.
Asa Smith, Brookfield.
Lebbeus Smith, Medfield.
Samuel Smith, jun. Walpole.
John Shepard, Foxborough.
David Southworth, Ward.
Oliver Shepard, Stoughton.
Gordon Strobridge, Northfield, (Ver.)
Miss Lucinda Smith, Norton.

### T

Doct. Ezra Thayer, Swanzey, (N. H.)
Daniel Thurber, Mendon.
Mr. Alvan Tobey, R. I. College.
James Tallmadge, jun. Do.
James Thompson, Do.
Allen Tillinghast, Merchant, Wrentham.
Aaron Thomas, Boylston.

U

Mr. Alvan Underwood, R. I. College.
Jonathan Upham, Stoughton.

W

Rev. William Williams, Wrentham.
Mr. Edmund T. Waring, R. I. College.
Conrade Webb, Do.

William H. Williams, Do.
————————Witherspoon, Do.
Nathaniel Willis, Boston.
Joseph Ware, Medway.
Obed Wheelock, Milford.
Abner Wight, Do.
Moses Woodman, Byfield.
Miss Hannah Wight, Foxborough.

The following were returned too late to be inserted in order.

Capt. John Bliss, Springfield.
Lieut. Samuel Bolter, Northampton.
Mr. John Breck, Merchant, Do.
Mrs. Sarah Chandler, Boston.
Jonathan Dwight, Att. at Law, Springfield.
Benjamin A. Edwards, Q. M. Northampton.
Mr. William Ely, Springfield.
  Daniel Fay, Westbury.
Jonathan Grout, Att. at Law, Belcherstown.
Ebenezer Hunt, jun. M.D. Northampton.
Mr. David Hunt, Merchant, Do.
  Jacob Hunt, Do.
  William Hutchens, Do.
  John W. Hooker, Springfield.

Mr. James Ingols, Northampton.
  Samuel King, jun. Do.
Levi Lyman, Esq. Do.
Maj. Samuel Lyman, Do.
Daniel Lombard, Merchant, Springfield.
Lieut. Moses Parsons, jun. Northampton.
Mr. Seth Pomeroy, Do.
  Nathaniel Patten, Hartford.
Doct. George Rogers, Northampton.
Solomon Stoddard, Esq. Do.
Mr. Nathan Stores, Do.
  Levi Shepard, Merchant, Do.
  Charles Steele, Boston.
  Caleb Smith, Hadley.

Mr. Jacob Wicker, Northampton.

**INDEX**

# INDEX

Her military equipments, 97. First encounter with the enemy, 100. Wounded, 101. Campaign in Virginia, 106-110. Her lover visits the camp in search of her, 153-163. Her (supposed) letter to her mother, 117, 138-150. Another encounter with the enemy, 119. Wounded, 120. Narrowly escapes the discovery of her sex, 161. Captures fifteen Tories at Vantassel's house, 125. Scouting parties, 100. In great danger, 121. Winter expedition to the head waters of the Hudson, 128. Gen. Schuyler, 129. She becomes waiter to Gen. Paterson, 130. Cessation of hostilities, 131. Journey to the Clove, 169. Bathing in the river, 133. Seized with malignant fever in Philadelphia, 135. Discovery of her sex, 136. A love-adventure, 153-163. Interview with the *inamorata*, 152. Tour in the unsettled parts of Virginia, 141-51. Adventures with the Indians, 141-51. Kills an Indian, 148. In great danger, 149. Supposed reflections in immediate prospect of death, 150. Returns to Philadelphia, 152. Dr. Binney gives her a letter to Gen. Paterson, disclosing her sex, 156. Narrowly escapes drowning in New-York Bay, 156. Arrives at West Point, 95, 157. Her sex becomes known to Gen. Paterson and Col. Jackson, 157. Her discharge from the army, 160. Returns to Massachusetts, 161. Her first winter after leaving the army, 161. Her marriage, 162. Her subsequent history and death, 163. Her person described, 97 .Appearance before the public in Boston Theatre, 164. Mrs. Gannett in 1820, 163-4. Obituary notice, 166. Gravestone, 165. Further notices, 163-6.

Scammell, Col. Alexander, 106.
Schools in New England in 1780, 74.
Schuyler, Gen., 129.
Semiramis, 24.
Shepard, Col. William 12, 14, 16, 18. Account of him, 96.

Siege of Boston, 65. Of Yorktown, 106.
Sing Sing skirmish near, 100.
Smith, Mrs., a heroine, 23.
Snow, Richard, sick, 123. Dies, 124.
Southworth, Alice, 36.
Sperin, Noble, killed, 102.
Sproat, Earle, 90.
Sproat, Col. Ebenezer, 101.
Sproat, James, 18.
Standish, Alexander, 35. Lydia, *ib.* Miles, *ib.*
Swan, Mrs., of Boston, 103.

T.

Tarrytown, action at, 13, 14, 16, 18, 100, 101, 122.
Thacher, Dr. James, author of "The Military Journal," 103, 108, 109, 110, 113, 115, 126. Mr. Mann borrows largely from him, 103, 115, 126.
Thacher, Rev. Peter, 41. Rev. Thomas, *ib.*
Thomas, Benjamin, 41. Anecdote of him, *ib.* His character, 46.
Thomas, Jeremiah, 54.
Thorp, Capt. Eliphalet, 18. His certificate, 19, 95, 99.
Treaty of Peace, 159.
Tupper, Col. Benjamin, account of him, 140.

U.

Uxbridge, 19, 94.

V.

Vantassel, a Tory, 123-125

W.

Warren, Gen. Joseph, at Bunker Hill, 66, 68.
Waterloo, 23.
Webb, Capt. George, 12, 14, 16, 18, 96, 100.
White Plains, 100.
Wood, Israel, 90.

Y.

"Yankee," origin of the term, 109.
Yorktown besieged, 106. Taken, 110

Made in the USA
Middletown, DE
10 March 2020